Vo

The *L*IFE of DAVID

CLARENCE SEXTON

CROWN
CHRISTIAN
PUBLICATIONS
Royal Reading

FAITHFORTHEFAMILY.COM

Volume 1

The Life of David

First Edition
Copyright
January 2006

CROWN
CHRISTIAN
PUBLICATIONS
Royal Reading

FAITHFORTHEFAMILY.COM

THE LIFE OF DAVID, VOLUME 1

Copyright © 2006
Crown Christian Publications
Powell, Tennessee 37849
CrownChristianPublications.com
FaithfortheFamily.com
ISBN: 1-58981-282-4

Layout by Stephen Troell

Printed in the United States of America

Dedication

This book is dedicated to Stephen Troell. Stephen is an outstanding young man who has worked very hard in a way that honors the Lord to lay out and design each of my books. God bless you, Stephen.

Clarence Axton

Acts 5:42

Contents

CHAPTER ONE

GOD FOUND HIS MAN

ur faith is a treasured heritage, and there are defining moments in our faith that allow us to catch a glimpse of God's heart. At this point in the Bible, as we enter the story of God's unfolding drama of redemption we become aquainted with a most remarkable man. His name is Samuel. The Lord called him and prepared him to be a prophet during one of the most tragic times in the history of God's people.

During the reign of King Saul, the prophet Samuel became extremely heavy-hearted over the condition of the kingdom, and in particular, over what he knew to be true concerning Israel's rebellion. God had rejected Saul. Israel desperately needed leadership. Something had to be done. The man of God had a broken heart as he thought about his nation. Saul was the people's choice. He was the best of the flesh, but we are going to learn that God always gives His best to those who leave the choice with Him. The Lord revealed to Samuel that His man had been found. In our story, we learn more concerning the heart of God than we learn about the heart of men.

In I Samuel 16:1 we read,

> And the LORD said unto Samuel, How long wilt thou mourn for Saul, seeing I have rejected him from reigning over Israel? fill thine horn with oil, and go, I will send thee to Jesse the Bethlehemite: for I have provided me a king among his sons.

David, the son of Jesse, was God's chosen king. David is mentioned 1,127 times in the Bible. By way of comparison, the apostle Paul is mentioned 163 times in the Bible. Just a handful of chapters are given to Abraham and Joseph. However, fifty-four chapters of the Bible are given to the life of David, not including the Psalms.

> *God always gives His best to those who leave the choice with Him.*

Our God has placed an unmistakable emphasis on the life of David. What is there about this man that God wants us to know that is so vital that He speaks of him over a thousand times in His Word?

In I Samuel 16:1 God announced, *"I have provided me a king."* Then He instructed Samuel in verse three, *"Thou shalt anoint unto me him whom I name unto thee."*

The Lord did a wonderful work in David's life to enable him to lead his generation. God said, *"I have provided me a king."*

The Lord still searches for those He can bless and use. He is searching this very moment for those who have a heart for Him. He sees what men do not see. He looks where men cannot look. He spies out our spiritual lives and sees what is in our hearts. I Samuel 16:7 says, *"But the LORD said unto Samuel, Look not on his*

countenance, or on the height of his stature; because I have refused him: for the LORD seeth not as man seeth; for man looketh on the outward appearance, but the LORD looketh on the heart."

An often overlooked principle unfolds in this Bible scene. It is that God begins something long before men ever see evidence of it. Saul had been rejected long before the people saw it because God saw in the heart of Saul something that He could not bless. In the same way, David had been chosen long before the nation of Israel ever recognized him because God found what He could bless in the heart of David.

God raises up people to do mighty things. He searches for those who have a heart for Him. God has already made a plan to bless in an outstanding way, a way that is far beyond what we ordinarily witness. He is still looking. Oh, how we should desire God to find what He is looking for in our lives!

In every town and every village, in every city and every church, in every part of the country and in every country of the world, God is searching the hearts of people. God is looking in your neighborhood; He is looking in your workplace. The Lord is looking in your school. He is looking for someone to bless and use. Do you want to be one of those people? If you do and if you desire God with all your heart, I promise you, God will find you and bless you and use you.

All of us are doing as much for God as we desire to do. All of us are at the stage in our Christian lives where we desire to be. We are content to be what we are. We do not go any further with the Lord until we have a desire to do so. God can work in our hearts to create that desire.

THE LORD IS IN CONTROL

It appeared to Samuel that the kingdom was out of control. Saul's life was certainly out of control, but God was still in control. We seem to have the idea that when things around us are falling apart, the whole world must be coming apart at the seams as well.

When we see families torn apart or experience difficulties in our own lives or in the life of the church that we are attending, we need to be reminded that God is still in control. The reins of the universe are still in His hands.

In Philippians 4:5 Paul exhorted believers, *"Let your moderation be known unto all men. The Lord is at hand."* Some think this verse simply means that the Lord is always near. Others believe that this verse means the Lord's return is near. Both are true. The Lord is near and the Lord's return is near. *"The Lord is at hand."* Our God is always near enough to do the work He chooses to do.

> *All of us are doing as much for God as we desire to do.*

He continues in Philippians 4:6-7, *"Be careful for nothing; but in every thing by prayer and supplication with thanksgiving let your requests be made known unto God. And the peace of God, which passeth all understanding, shall keep your hearts and minds through Christ Jesus."*

If we will remember that *"the Lord is at hand,"* then we can *"be careful for nothing."* Most often, when we quote this passage we quote verses six and seven together and leave out verse five. However, we are not going to be able to obey the command of verse six if we leave out verse five. In order for us not to worry, we must realize that *"the Lord is at hand."* When we realize this, we can *"be careful for nothing."* We need not worry about anything because God is in control.

As an old man, Samuel carried a crushing burden. Remember that Hannah, Samuel's mother, prayed before he was born that God would give her a son. She promised the Lord that she would give that son back to Him. Dedicated to God before his birth, Samuel's whole

12

life had been given to serving the Lord. He even established a school of prophets to train men to serve the Lord.

However, the people had asked for a king. Samuel, as their spiritual leader, felt he had been rejected. Israel wanted to be like every other nation. God granted their request, and Saul came to reign as king in Israel.

Everything the old prophet had given his life to accomplish seemed to be in vain. He was greatly troubled. In a loving rebuke, God spoke to him in the first verse of I Samuel 16, *"How long wilt thou mourn for Saul?"* In so many words, "Samuel, how long are you going to be upset about this? How long will you live without trusting God in this matter?"

We all have people and things that are difficult to give to God. However, it is not that we cannot; it is that we will not. You may not trust your loved ones to do the right thing; however, you must trust God to do the right thing with those loved ones. Final surrender to God does not necessarily mean that God is going to move in a flash to do something; but it does mean that the moment we commit it to God, He will give us peace in knowing that He will take care of it.

God asked Samuel, "How long will you worry and fret? How long will you think that this is your nation and your people and not My nation and My people?" Many times the Lord has said to me, "How long will you think that this is your church and these are your people?" The church is the Lord's, and these are His people. It is His work.

As I yield my life to God and give my children to the Lord, realizing they are a gift from Him, I find a wonderful peace in Him. Realizing that God is in control brings such comfort to my heart.

God said in I Samuel 16:1, *"How long wilt thou mourn for Saul, seeing I have rejected him from reigning over Israel?"*

The Lord commanded Samuel to travel to Bethlehem to anoint a king. He said to Samuel, "Make the journey to Jesse's house. I have found a king. I want you to anoint him." There can never be doubt about this fact, God is in control!

THE LORD IS ALWAYS WORKING

We may not always see God's work, but He is always working. He was preparing David when no one knew much about him except the Lord. If you read carefully the sixteenth chapter, you will see that God dealt with Samuel, then Jesse, then Jesse's sons, then finally God dealt with David. God dealt with each one in a different way.

> *You may not trust your loved ones to do the right thing; however, you must trust God to do the right thing with those loved ones.*

Full of worry and fretting, Samuel had to learn that God was in control. Of his eight sons and two daughters, Jesse surely believed that God would use one of his children. And He was just as certain that David was not the one. When seven of his sons were rejected and the horn of oil was not poured on them, God had to deal with them.

Finally, the Lord was at work in David's life. David was a shepherd. He had the heart of a shepherd. Later we read that he was willing to risk his life and to give his life, if necessary, for one of his sheep. God was doing something in the life of this shepherd boy, for God is always at work.

The Lord told the old prophet, "Go down to Jesse's house." Samuel said, "I can't go; Saul will kill me." God said, "You tell him that you are going to offer a sacrifice. Meet with Jesse and his family alone. Have his sons brought before you, and I will show you that I have provided Myself a king."

Jesse's sons were brought before Samuel. Seven of his sons appeared, but the eighth was still out tending the sheep. One by one they came before Samuel and God said, "That's not the one; that's not the one; that's not the one." Finally, when they had all passed, Samuel said to Jesse, "Are all of your sons here?"

We doubt that great things can be done. Recently, I read of a man conducting experiments with fish. He placed a large fish in a tank along with several minnows. The large fish consumed all the minnows. Then, he put more minnows inside the tank, but within a glass enclosure. The fish would attempt to attack them, but he could not get to them. Finally, the man released the minnows from the enclosure. But, the large fish would not move. He had learned that he could not get to them, so he would no longer even try. The fish had been conditioned to believe that it could not be done. So many of God's children have come to believe that "it" cannot be done.

We allow our minds to be conditioned to believe that God is not going to do great things. We think, "God may work somewhere else, but He is not going to work here." But God is always working. We should desire for God to do a mighty work in our lives and in the lives of our families and churches.

THE LORD USES PEOPLE OTHERS OVERLOOK

Samuel said to Jesse, "Are these all your boys?" He said, "I have another young son in the field keeping the sheep." Because Jesse was able to send someone else to replace David to care for the sheep, he could have already brought David in from the field had he thought that God might use him.

Knowing David and the heart he had for God, can you imagine how he would have loved to have been in that meeting with Samuel?

He would have thought it the greatest privilege of his life to be there when the prophet Samuel came on his journey from Ramah. But, he was overlooked and forgotten.

> *Because Jesse was able to send someone else to replace David to care for the sheep, he could have already brought David in from the field had he thought that God might use him.*

Many things must have gone through the mind of Samuel on his journey to Bethlehem. Now, thinking that he had seen all of Jesse's sons but one and knowing that God had said one of Jesse's sons was to be the king, can you imagine how Samuel felt as he was waiting for David to arrive? Finally, David arrived at the house. Face to face stood the young shepherd with the prophet. "This is My king," Samuel heard God say. Hands trembling with excitement, Samuel reached inside his garment for the anointing oil, and David, standing there before his father and his brethren, was anointed by Samuel to be king over Israel. The oil ran from David's body and dripped to the ground. David was only in his teens. Years would pass before he would actually reign as king of Israel.

God uses people others have overlooked. This is what Paul meant when he wrote in I Corinthians 1:26-29,

> *For ye see your calling, brethren, how that not many wise men after the flesh, not many mighty, not many noble, are called: but God hath chosen the foolish things of the world to confound the wise; and God hath chosen the weak things of the world to confound the things which are mighty; and base things of the world, and things which are despised, hath God chosen, yea, and things which are not, to*

bring to nought things that are: that no flesh should glory in his presence.

God works in such a way that He gets the glory. If we begin to steal His glory, He will stop blessing. The glory belongs to the Lord, not to men. Salvation is the starting point, and God desires to finish the work that He has started in all our lives. *"Being confident of this very thing, that he which hath begun a good work in you will perform it until the day of Jesus Christ"* (Philippians 1:6).

Recently, my wife and I were in a fast-food restaurant and a lady and her young boy, just a short distance away, caught my attention. I do not think the child had any idea that I was watching him and his mother, but as my mind traveled back to my childhood, I could see myself standing there with my mother. My mind was flooded with memories. I recognized him, and I felt that he probably recognized me because he attended our church. On the way out, the mother spoke to me and said, "Hello, Pastor Sexton." I greeted the mother and her son.

As that boy stood there with his mother, perhaps he thought, "This is my pastor. He is someone special, someone important." Maybe he started thinking about himself. However, God sees things far differently than we do. When that child passed by me, I could not help thinking, "He may be the next pastor of our church."

Dear friend, think what God did with a shepherd boy. The Lord said to David, *"I took thee from the sheepcote, from following the sheep, to be ruler over my people, over Israel"* (II Samuel 7:8). There is a God in heaven who desires to bless and use us. Allow Him to bless and use you.

CHAPTER TWO

THE KING'S CLASSROOM

avid was a mighty man of God. God gives much attention to him in His Word. The name of David is mentioned 1,127 times in the Bible. Our Lord devotes fifty-four chapters of Scripture, not including many of the Psalms, to this man.

The sixteenth chapter of the book of I Samuel is easily divided into halves. The first half tells the story about the prophet Samuel going to Bethlehem to anoint a king. What a sight to see the prophet of God coming down the road into the village of Bethlehem. He was coming on divine orders to find the next king of Israel and anoint him. He arrived at the house of Jesse who was of the tribe of Judah.

The sons of Jesse were brought before him. As Samuel saw seven of the sons, God said to him, "I have not chosen these." Samuel turned to Jesse and asked, *"Are here all thy children?"* Jesse told Samuel that he had one more boy who was tending the sheep. The prophet told Jesse that they could do nothing else until David arrived.

As David stood before Samuel, Samuel heard the voice of God saying, "This is My king." He reached within his garment, took out the horn of oil, and poured it on David's head. David stood there with oil dripping from his body, having been anointed king.

However, another king sat on the throne of Israel; his name was Saul. It would be nearly fifteen years before David would sit on the throne of Israel. At this point, God begins to tell us how He prepared David for the throne.

In the last half of chapter sixteen, the scene changes from Bethlehem where Samuel stood with David and his family, back to Saul and to what was taking place in the palace of the king. The Bible says in I Samuel 16:14-23,

> *But the Spirit of the LORD departed from Saul, and an evil spirit from the LORD troubled him. And Saul's servants said unto him, Behold now, an evil spirit from God troubleth thee. Let our lord now command thy servants, which are before thee, to seek out a man, who is a cunning player on an harp: and it shall come to pass, when the evil spirit from God is upon thee, that he shall play with his hand, and thou shalt be well. And Saul said unto his servants, Provide me now a man that can play well, and bring him to me. Then answered one of the servants, and said, Behold, I have seen a son of Jesse the Bethlehemite, that is cunning in playing, and a mighty valiant man, and a man of war, and prudent in matters, and a comely person, and the LORD is with him. Wherefore Saul sent messengers unto Jesse, and said, Send me David thy son, which is with the sheep. And Jesse took an ass laden with bread, and a bottle of wine, and a kid, and sent them by David his son unto Saul. And David came to Saul, and stood before him: and he loved him greatly; and he became his armour-bearer. And Saul*

sent to Jesse, saying, Let David, I pray thee, stand before me; for he hath found favour in my sight. And it came to pass, when the evil spirit from God was upon Saul, that David took an harp, and played with his hand: so Saul was refreshed, and was well, and the evil spirit departed from him.

Remember, David had been anointed king. This was the first of the three times in David's life that he would be anointed. Even though David was to be king of Israel, there were special things that God had to do in David's life before he reached the throne.

As we look at this portion of Scripture, note one expression that to us seems unlikely in the matter of preparation. The Bible says in verse twenty-one, *"And David came to Saul, and stood before him."*

David came into the king's classroom. Where does a shepherd boy learn to be king? He learns in the king's classroom. Where is God working in your life? What does the Lord have for you to do? God did not place us on planet Earth without purpose. There is not one man or woman

> *There is not one man or woman who is insignificant to God.*

who is insignificant to God. God has a chosen plan for each of us. He has a blueprint with your name on it. There is an unconscious preparation going on in your life at this moment.

How does God go about working in our lives to accomplish His purpose? Did you ever think that disappointments you have faced this past week, or even this day, may have been from God? Did you ever think that someone you may be greatly disappointed in, or someone you may be greatly encouraged by may be a messenger from God? If there is a God in heaven who made us and placed us here with purpose, then we should also understand that God is working in all things to accomplish His purpose in our lives.

David entered into the king's classroom. He was brought from the field, where he was tending the sheep, to the court of the king because he was headed some day to the throne of Israel. It was time to "school" the future king. There are helpful things that we need to understand about this king's classroom.

> *Our God gives instruction to the obedient heart.*

I do not know what your memories of school are, but my memories are of an uneasy start. I lived in Selma, Alabama, when I started school. Although I was nearly six, I was enrolled in a private kindergarten. That did not last long. We were constantly on the move from one town to the next.

My first grade experience lasted only six weeks. At the end of six weeks, my mother and father decided that I was too sick to go to school. Some of the teachers agreed. It was not because I had been deviant; but I was considered to be too ill, nervous, and frustrated. We had lived in about ten different places up until that time, so it was not too big of a surprise that I was a "sickly" first grader.

After being withdrawn from school, I stayed home for the rest of that year. We then moved to another part of the country. It came time to enroll in the second grade, and my brother and I were to attend school together. We started out one fine morning and my frustrated father announced to us that he was turning his car around and we were going to stay at home for the entire school year. It sounded great to us! Just as my dad said, we did not go to school a single day that entire year.

When it came time to start school the next year, we had moved to another place. This time my mother took the responsibility of getting us to school. I never shall forget that day when we walked to Sam Houston School in Maryville, Tennessee. My mother marched into the principal's office with two boys by her side, and Mr. Howard asked her, "What grade are these boys in, Mrs. Sexton?" She said without hesitation, "They are both third graders." It was both a surprise and a relief!

We had only been to school six weeks in the first grade; we had not been to school at all in the second grade; now we were about to start to class in the third grade. We were led off to the third grade classroom and to a teacher who was teaching her first year. She had never been married. She was a tall, lovely, redheaded lady whose name was Miss Burns. I learned to love her because she demonstrated such love to me.

> *Remove all secondary causes in your life and by faith see the hand of God at work.*

My brother lasted two weeks in the third grade. I remember the sad day when the principal came to the teacher, and they both sat my brother down and said, "Tommy, you are not ready for this." They took him to the second grade. I stayed in the third grade and finished my third grade year. From then on things got much better. It is truly amazing to realize how our God guides our lives.

The Instructor

As we look into the king's classroom, we discover some of the same things at work in David's life. The instructor, I want you to notice, was none other than the Lord. The Bible says that the Lord was with David. The Bible says in verse thirteen, *"Then Samuel took the horn of oil, and anointed him in the midst of his brethren: and the Spirit of the LORD came upon David from that day forward. So Samuel rose up, and went to Ramah."*

David's instructor was the Holy Spirit. The Lord taught David as his life was yielded to God. God will use anything at His disposal to teach us what He wants us to learn. Our God gives instruction to the obedient heart.

If you pay close attention, you will understand that the Spirit of God is teaching us things today and every day. There are lessons we learn as He speaks to us through His Word, through circumstances, and through other Christians. Remove all secondary causes in your life and by faith see the hand of God at work.

The Pupil

King Saul had become very troubled, and those closest to him knew that something was terribly wrong. They had been hearing him and watching him, and they knew that an evil spirit had come to him. The Lord allowed this because of Saul's disobedience.

> *Get hold of the fact that the Spirit of God desires to be your daily teacher.*

Saul's servants gathered around him and said, "We want to help you." I think they should have said, "You need to repent of your sins. Seek out the prophet Samuel and get right with God. Ask God to bless you and your kingdom." But they said, "We believe that music would help you. We would like to find someone who can play beautifully and soothe your troubled heart." When they knew that the king thought it was a good idea, one of them got up enough courage to speak. He said, "I know someone who can play for you."

In verse eighteen we read that he told the king seven things about this person. We should make special note of them.

First he said this young man was *"a son of Jesse the Bethlehemite."* This identified him. It identified his tribe, his heritage, his family, and the place of his upbringing.

Second, he said of this pupil that he was *"cunning in playing."* He played beautifully on the harp.

Third, he said that he was *"a mighty valiant man."* David was the mightiest hero of the Old Testament, yet he could sit down and play an instrument beautifully. What a wonderful combination of strength and beauty!

Fourth he said that he was *"a man of war."* David was willing to fight. He was not simply someone who talked about it; he had courage.

Fifth he said he was *"prudent in matters."* David had good judgment. He could make right decisions.

Sixth he was *"a comely person."* He was very pleasing in appearance. The way he looked and the way he behaved himself was beautiful to behold.

Seventh and most important he said, *"The LORD is with him."* It is significant that the Bible says of David, *"The LORD is with him,"* and the Bible says of Saul in I Samuel 16:14, *"The Spirit of the LORD departed from Saul."*

We have seen the instructor and the pupil in the king's classroom, so the stage is set. The Bible says, *"The LORD is with him."* This means David knew the Lord personally. If you know the Lord personally, if you have asked God to forgive your sin, and by faith you have received Jesus Christ as your Savior, the Lord is with you. He is constantly working in your life. What is He attempting to accomplish in you? What lessons do we find God teaching us today?

I hope you have asked the Lord to forgive your sin. I hope that by faith you have received the Lord Jesus as your Savior. If you have, get hold of the fact that the Spirit of God desires to be your daily teacher. You are the pupil, and He is the teacher. Everything around you becomes a classroom.

THE LESSON OF SUBMISSION TO AUTHORITY

God was teaching David the lesson of submission to authority. The Bible says David was already a man of war. He was already mighty, valiant, and prudent in matters; but when David's father said, "You go to Saul," David went to Saul. He was being taught the lesson of submission to authority.

> *If there is a greater lesson we need to learn in life than the lesson of submission to authority, I do not know what that lesson would be.*

I have met many people who cannot lead and will not follow. If they cannot lead, and their inability to lead is connected to their unwillingness to follow, God cannot bless and use those people.

If there is a greater lesson we need to learn in life than the lesson of submission to authority, I do not know what that lesson would be. God wants us to yield ourselves to Him, to place our lives under His mighty hand. David was learning these lessons of obedience and submission. If one is going to teach, he must remain teachable. If one is going to lead, he must continue to be willing to follow. Our leadership is provided as we follow the leading of our Lord.

You and I know if we have yielded our hearts to God. If I am not yielded in my heart, it makes no difference how well I might speak or what I might say. I will not have God's blessing if I am not yielded to Him.

In I Samuel 15, God told Saul to obey Him, but Saul did not obey. In the closing part of verse eleven the Bible says, *"And it grieved Samuel; and he cried unto the LORD all night."* Saul was not obedient or submissive. Samuel said to Saul in verse twenty-three that Saul's

26

rebellion and stubbornness was as the sin of witchcraft. Incidentally, that is where Saul ended up, with a witch. If you think that lack of submission is not a serious matter, God says that it is as witchcraft.

Samuel also said, *"Stubbornness is as iniquity and idolatry."* Why is stubbornness as idolatry? It is as iniquity and idolatry because when we are not yielded to God, we are worshipping self.

David had to go to the king's classroom. He looked at the life of Saul every day, and he saw in Saul a man filled with evil. He saw that the Spirit of God had departed from him. He knew that because of Saul's rebellion and pride, God had taken His hand off his life. No doubt David thought, "Oh, I never want that to happen to me."

If you read I Samuel 15, you will find that the old prophet Samuel was so disturbed about what Saul refused to do that when King Agag had been captured and not killed, Samuel himself said, "Bring King Agag to me." He took the sword in his own hand, and the Bible says, *"And Samuel hewed Agag in pieces before the Lord"* (I Samuel 15:33). He believed that God's orders must be obeyed. You may not understand that. You do not have to understand it; but you should read it and believe it.

> *If one is going to teach, he must remain teachable.*

This reminds us how serious a matter it is to obey God. David had to go to school. He went to school in the king's classroom to learn the lesson of submission to authority. Saul became an example of a bad pupil who would not submit. To David, he was a constant reminder of what his life would be like if he did not yield to God. You may know someone who is a constant reminder of what your life is going to be like if you do not yield to God. It seems that the only purpose some people serve is to provide a bad example of what we never want to be.

THE LESSON OF SAFETY

Samuel thought on the way to David's house, "If Saul finds out what is going on, in his anger, he will kill me." Saul had no idea that David had been anointed king over Israel. Is it not interesting that God took David right to the place where his life would be in the most jeopardy? He proved to David that He could take care of him in what we would think of as the most unsafe place in the world.

It seems that the only purpose some people serve is to provide a bad example of what we never want to be.

You who know the Bible and know David's life, know something of what David would have to deal with in the future. Later, Saul took three thousand choice soldiers and hunted David like a wild beast. David had to trust God to keep him safe. Can you see that David needed to learn the lesson of safety? The Lord is the One who keeps us safe from all harm. God takes care of His children.

In Psalm 54 David cried out,

> *Save me, O God, by thy name, and judge me by thy strength. Hear my prayer, O God; give ear to the words of my mouth. For strangers are risen up against me, and oppressors seek after my soul: they have not set God before them. Selah. Behold, God is mine helper: the Lord is with them that uphold my soul. He shall reward evil unto mine enemies: cut them off in thy truth. I will freely sacrifice unto thee: I will praise thy name, O LORD; for it is good. For he hath delivered me out of all trouble: and mine eye hath seen his desire upon mine enemies.*

David learned the lesson of safety. God wants us to learn the lesson of trusting Him for our safety. David wrote in Psalm 20:7, *"Some trust in chariots, some in horses: but we will remember the name of the LORD our God."*

THE LESSON OF SINGLENESS OF PURPOSE

By the expression "singleness of purpose," I mean that all things God does in our lives are connected to one another. Why did Samuel go to anoint David? Samuel was a bridge between the prophets and the kings. Samuel was a common denominator between Saul and David. Samuel was the man of God chosen to speak to both Saul and David.

Why did a servant speak up with David's name when Saul needed help? Were there not other men who could play the harp? Were there not others who could go to the king's palace and soothe the king's troubled soul? Why did God give David favor with that servant? It is because all things God does in a man's life are connected to one another. His way is perfect!

Samuel was a bridge between the prophets and the kings.

David was sent to the palace with the king to see how a king conducts himself. He was to see who the king's mighty warriors were. He needed to learn something about the king's family and the king's ways, because David was going to be the king.

Have you lived long enough to see how some things that have happened to you in the past are being used of God in your life today? Have you lived long enough to see how some tragedy that you faced has been used of God to help you comfort someone else who is going through the same thing? Have you lived long enough to see how some disappointment you have dealt with has been used of God to allow you to help someone else who is dealing with the same disappointment? Have you lived long enough to see that some difficult person you had to deal with early in life enabled you to deal with someone like that or even more difficult? We must learn the lesson of singleness of purpose.

God is at work. What He is doing today works together with what He did yesterday and what He will do tomorrow. There are lessons to learn here. We learn by faith to trust God in submission. We say, "Lord, Your way is the best way." We learn by faith to trust God for safety, and we learn by faith to trust God for singleness of purpose. When we learn these lessons, we find a gentle, sweet peace as we lean on the Lord.

Some people go to school, but never learn their lessons.

Some people go to school, but never learn their lessons. David says again in Psalm 57:1-2, *"Be merciful unto me, O God, be merciful unto me: for my soul trusteth in thee: yea, in the shadow of thy wings will I make my refuge, until these calamities be overpast. I will cry unto God most high; unto God that performeth all things for me."* David said, "I have lived to learn that God is doing all these things for me."

My heart has been broken, and I have said, "Oh God, why?" Later I learned that if my heart had not been broken, I would have gone a direction that was not God's choosing for my life. I would have put my confidence in unfaithful people.

As God's pupils, we have a lesson to learn about submission, a lesson to learn about safety, and a lesson to learn about singleness of purpose. Let us be Christians, and be good students, so that when the grades are passed out at the end of life's semester, we will receive top grades on the subjects that God is teaching us.

CHAPTER THREE

GOD HAS A CHAMPION

 ne of the most beloved and well-known stories of all the Bible is the story of David and Goliath. In the valley of Elah, the armies of Israel and the armies of the Philistines had set themselves in array. For forty days, a massive man over nine feet tall stood and called out to the army of Israel, taunting them to send a champion to face him. Why, among all the thousands of people who lived in David's day, did God choose David to do battle with Goliath? Why was it David? In this perilous hour in which we live, we need more people like David.

The Bible says in I Samuel 17:1-14,

> *Now the Philistines gathered together their armies to battle, and were gathered together at Shochoh, which belongeth to Judah, and pitched between Shochoh and Azekah, in Ephes-dammim. And Saul and the men of Israel were gathered together, and pitched by the*

*valley of Elah, and set the battle in array against the
Philistines. And the Philistines stood on a mountain
on the one side, and Israel stood on a mountain on
the other side: and there was a valley between them.
And there went out a champion out of the camp of the
Philistines, named Goliath, of Gath, whose height
was six cubits and a span. And he had an helmet of
brass upon his head, and he was armed with a coat
of mail; and the weight of the coat was five thousand
shekels of brass. And he had greaves of brass upon
his legs, and a target of brass between his shoulders.
And the staff of his spear was like a weaver's beam;
and his spear's head weighed six hundred shekels of
iron: and one bearing a shield went before him. And
he stood and cried unto the armies of Israel, and said
unto them, Why are ye come out to set your battle in
array? am not I a Philistine, and ye servants to Saul?
choose you a man for you, and let him come down
to me. If he be able to fight with me, and to kill me,
then will we be your servants: but if I prevail against
him, and kill him, then shall ye be our servants, and
serve us. And the Philistine said, I defy the armies
of Israel this day; give me a man, that we may fight
together. When Saul and all Israel heard those words
of the Philistine, they were dismayed, and greatly
afraid. Now David was the son of that Ephrathite
of Bethlehem-judah, whose name was Jesse; and he
had eight sons: and the man went among men for an
old man in the days of Saul. And the three eldest sons
of Jesse went and followed Saul to the battle: and the
names of his three sons that went to the battle were
Eliab the firstborn, and next unto him Abinadab, and
the third Shammah. And David was the youngest:
and the three eldest followed Saul.*

The battle was about to take place, and the Philistines decided that they would set the terms. As we observe this Philistine giant and how God dealt with him, we learn much about how the Lord works. I desire the Lord to work in my life and in the life the church I pastor.

When my family and I were in Paterson, New Jersey, a few miles from New York City, we lived in a neighborhood where one of the basketball players for the New York Knicks lived. He was a professing Christian, and I made acquaintance with him. One day he came to our school gymnasium, and he wanted to give a speech to our boys in gym class. I told him to help himself. I found out later that he usually charged thousands of dollars to give that same speech. That day it was free.

Why, among all the thousands of people who lived in David's day, did God choose David to do battle with Goliath?

When he walked in, all the boys knew who he was and they stood at attention with their eyes fastened on him. He gathered them together and said, "I am going to tell you how I got to be a professional basketball player. I made it to the top, T-O-P. It takes three things to get to the top. First, T–it takes talent. You must have it. Some people have more than others, but you have to have it. Secondly, O–it takes opportunity. Some folks are never given the opportunity. I have been given the opportunity. The third thing, which is most important, is P–you must have persistence. You have to stay at it. Some people have the talent, some have the opportunity, but they don't have the persistence. They don't stay at it."

It was a nice speech, and I thought the kids enjoyed hearing it; but if we are not careful, this is how we will approach the Christian life. Most Christians I know would believe this is the way to live the Christian life. They think all that matters is educating and helping the flesh to function better. Is there nothing more?

As we read through I Samuel 17, we read all these things about the Philistines and Goliath; then suddenly, God changes the scene. Remember that the Holy Spirit wrote this Book. He is the Author. The scene change is in verse twelve where God simply says, *"Now David was the son of that Ephrathite of Bethlehem-Judah."*

In other words, with all that was going on, the eyes of God were fastened on David. David had God's attention, and God had David's attention. Do you have God's attention? Does God have your attention? Are you that kind of person?

THE WORLD'S WAY

The world's way is might against might, army against army, and manpower against manpower. Their philosophy sounds simple, "I am going to outdo you." The Philistines had decided, after more than two decades of peace, that they were going to war. They were in the land that belonged to Judah. By the way, David was of the tribe of Judah. They set up their army on a hillside in plain view.

This story is for all people who love the Lord and want His blessing on their lives.

On my trips to the Holy Land, I have visited the valley of Elah many times. I have stood and imagined where David could have met Goliath. This massive man nearly ten feet tall came walking out of the crowd to confront David. One could tell even at a great distance that he was bigger than everyone else; but the closer he came, the bigger he seemed to be. If you read the story in I Samuel 17, you will find that he was covered with brass. The mid-eastern sun was beating down on that valley and glistening on that brass. There he stood shining like another sun. At his height he must have weighed between four hundred and five hundred pounds. He looked like some great, huge monster of a man.

Goliath cried out and said, "I defy the armies of God. Send somebody down here; we are going to have a fight. It is winner take all." The Bible says he did this for forty days. Can you imagine what it was like in the camp of the army of Israel after forty days of that?

The philosophy of this world without God is, "I'm going to push everyone around. I'm going to convince everyone with what I say. I'm going to get it done whatever it takes. I have the human ingenuity and ability to do whatever it takes to gain the victory. I intend to intimidate you."

David's relationship with God made him a champion.

We often have a philosophy, even in our churches, that all we need to do is pick ourselves up by the bootstraps and make things turn out the way we desire. The world's champion is the biggest, the brightest, the loudest, and the strongest.

THE LORD'S WAY

The Lord begins speaking of David in verse twelve of I Samuel 17. He does not describe his height, his weapons, or his armor. There is a reason for all this. God simply says, *"Now David was the son of that Ephrathite of Bethlehem-Judah."*

The Lord's way is not the world's way. Are you concerned about the Lord's way? This story is for all people who love the Lord and want His blessing on their lives. The Bible says in Isaiah 55:8-9, *"For my thoughts are not your thoughts, neither are your ways my ways, saith the Lord. For as the heavens are higher than the earth, so are my ways higher than your ways, and my thoughts than your thoughts."*

What is the Lord's way of doing things? The Lord's way was that young David was already prepared in private because of what he had in his heart. His relationship with God made him a champion.

Back in I Samuel 13:14, Samuel dealt with the sin of Saul and God's rejection of Saul. The Bible says,

> *But now thy kingdom shall not continue: the LORD hath sought him a man after his own heart, and the LORD hath commanded him to be captain over his people, because thou hast not kept that which the LORD commanded thee.*

> *David never sought to be king; he never planned to be king; he never tried to be king; he simply desired God. He loved God and wanted to be right with Him.*

God is always looking for someone who has a heart for Him. What is your motive? The only person the Lord will bless and use is the one whose motive is God alone. If you attempt to climb the ladder of success and leave God out, some day every rung will fall from beneath you.

David was the one who kept the sheep. David never sought to be king; he never planned to be king; he never tried to be king; he simply desired God. He loved God and wanted to be right with Him. In Acts 13:22 the Bible says, *"And when he had removed him, he raised up unto them David to be their king; to whom also he gave testimony, and said, I have found David the son of Jesse, a man after mine own heart, which shall fulfil all my will."*

When D. L. Moody was four years old living in Northfield, Massachusetts, his dad died and left the family bankrupt. That circumstance denied Moody a proper education. However, the

Encyclopedia Britannica says of D. L. Moody that he was the greatest evangelist of the nineteenth century. Why? Because God had His way in Moody's life. He found a man who had a heart for the Lord, and He used him and blessed him. I cannot make you think in a way that is after the heart of God, but I can tell you this is God's way. *"Man looketh on the outward appearance, but the LORD looketh on the heart"* (I Samuel 16:7).

WHAT WILL BE YOUR WAY?

Perhaps you have been manipulating, scheming, planning, and trying to convince someone what you can do. Come clean with God. What will be your way? It should be the way of coming to Jesus Christ and asking Him to forgive your sin, and by faith receiving Him as your Savior. Being born again is the starting place.

Knowing Jesus Christ as Savior does not make sense to the world. We can talk about "church" all we want to and not offend anyone; but if we confront someone about dying and going to hell, we find there is an offense to the gospel. This is the Lord's way. What is going to be our way? People need to hear that they are lost without God and without hope, and that Christ is the only way of salvation.

Coming to the Lord Jesus, yielding to Him, and saying, "Lord, take control,"

God has a champion. The strange thing is that we never know who that champion is until God calls him from the ranks of the unknown, overlooked, and insignificant, and works through that person's life.

should be our way. When I was eighteen years old, I said, "Lord, what You do with my life is Your business."

I remember standing in the yard with my mother-in-law when my wife and I and our two little boys were leaving Tennessee to pastor a church in New Jersey, eleven miles from New York City. One of my sons was getting ready to go into the fourth grade and the other was preparing to enter the seventh grade. They were going to face what we could never have imagined. I remember standing there crying, but knowing in my heart that this was God's way.

God has a champion. The strange thing is that we never know who that champion is until God calls him from the ranks of the unknown, overlooked, and insignificant, and works through that person's life. You could not pick the champion if you tried, because God looks on the heart. Be prepared for His service. Keep your heart right with Him.

Most people in the work of the Lord are always looking for the miraculous. They want to see some sudden display of divine favor they can tell about the remainder of their lives. On the contrary, our God takes the ordinary, the common place, the routine things and people in life and touches them with His mighty power. He brings forth the miraculous out of the ordinary. Be faithful to Him day by day. The miraculous is taking place already.

CHAPTER FOUR

IS THERE NOT A CAUSE?

he Bible is like no other book. It is the Word of God. The Bible provides more for us than the direct statements of our God; it records for us also the absolute perfect record of what others spoke. Among the recorded statements made by men and women in all of human history, one of the greatest is found in the story of David and Goliath. It is a question raised by David that places the highest motive on the right type of human behavior. It is a question that stirs our hearts to the core.

Look at the scene in the seventeenth chapter of the book of I Samuel. No greater distance than about three hundred yards separated the armies of Israel and of the Philistines. They were at the most narrow point of the valley of Elah. Gathered along the western slope was the Philistine army; along the eastern slope was the army of Israel. As David came upon the scene in the campsite, he was questioned and accused by his brother of having the wrong motive.

David responded by asking in I Samuel 17:29, *"What have I now done? Is there not a cause?"*

David said, *"Is there not a cause?* Is there not a reason to be here? Doesn't something need to be done?" The army of the Israelites had a leader, King Saul. Saul was a great physical specimen of a man. Why did he not do something?

There was no doubt that something needed to be done. The life of a nation was at stake. The Philistines were threatening them with a form of servitude. Someone needed to face this giant.

When David inquired about what was going on, it was his own brother who rebuked him. The Bible says in verse twenty-eight,

> *And Eliab his eldest brother heard when he spake unto the men; and Eliab's anger was kindled against David, and he said, Why camest thou down hither? and with whom hast thou left those few sheep in the wilderness? I know thy pride, and the naughtiness of thine heart; for thou art come down that thou mightest see the battle.*

In response to these accusations, David asked, *"What have I now done? Is there not a cause?"*

From the dawning of creation to the closing of the revelation of Jesus Christ when we see the final victory that God has given us in His Son, winding its way through all 1,189 chapters of the Bible, there is this cause. It is the cause of Christ. David found himself on that day in the valley of Elah doing his part, taking his turn, in this cause. We have a time, we have a turn, and we have a place in human history in this cause.

I do not live in some olden day that exists only in the pages of history. I am alive with opportunity to serve God in this day and hour. I must find my place in the cause of Christ.

If you read this story carefully and read what the king says in the seventeenth chapter, I think you will find it quite amusing at first and then sorrowful as you ponder it. In the thirty-seventh verse, where David has his interview with Saul, the Bible says,

> *David said moreover, The LORD that delivered me out of the paw of the lion, and out of the paw of the bear, he will deliver me out of the hand of this Philistine. And Saul said unto David, Go, and the LORD be with thee.*

In other words, he said to David, "I want you to go, and I want you to remember, the Lord be with you." That sounds so spiritual, does it not? Saul was doing all that talking about right things without reality. The Lord was not real to Saul. He knew the speech to make. He knew the words to say, but God was not real to him.

I am so troubled in my heart when I think that the majority of people in churches like ours know the right words to say, and the right speeches to make, but God is not real to them. We sit around and say things like, "Let's pray about it. Let's trust God. The Lord will be with you. God's Word has the answer." We use all those little phrases that we know to speak, but the truth is we are not speaking from the heart. May God deliver me from this pretense.

From the dawning of creation to the closing of the revelation of Jesus Christ when we see the final victory that God has given us in His Son, winding its way through all 1,189 chapters of the Bible, there is this cause. It is the cause of Christ.

Is God real to you today? My great fear is that I have been doing what I am doing long enough that I know what to do without doing

45

it in the strength of the Lord. I fear trying to do God's work without God's power. Saul was doing just that. He said, *"Go, and the LORD be with thee,"* and it sounded good.

Not long ago I remember talking to a man who was telling me how much he wanted God's blessing on his church, on his life, and on everything that he was doing. I learned later that while he was talking to me, he had been living in adultery for two years. He knew the speech, but he did not know the God of the speech.

> *I fear trying to do God's work without God's power.*

The king of Israel said, "Go, and God be with you," but God was not in the man's speech. We should examine our hearts and see if the fire is still burning. Is the fire still burning, or are we just going through the motions?

When David came on the scene, from his heart he said, *"Is there not a cause?"* The Lord Jesus Christ has given us His cause. Our Lord said in Matthew 28:19-20,

> *Go ye therefore, and teach all nations, baptizing them in the name of the Father, and of the Son, and of the Holy Ghost: teaching them to observe all things whatsoever I have commanded you: and, lo, I am with you alway, even unto the end of the world. Amen.*

David still had a pioneering spirit. He wanted to accomplish the mission God had given him.

HIS CAUSE WILL KEEP US ON THE RIGHT COURSE

We are all so easily sidetracked. Sometimes a thought or an idea comes to mind that de-emphasizes what God wants us to do. It grows a little larger until finally we are no longer doing what we once did for the Lord.

David came upon this scene and saw that his nation was in danger and about to be defeated. He saw that there was something that needed to be done. This was God's work and God's people and someone needed to stand up and do something about it.

Most people are not sidetracked with bad things. As a matter of fact, most good people are sidetracked with good things. They trade a good thing for the best thing God has given them to do. His cause will keep us on course. Are you still on course in your Christian life?

HIS CAUSE WILL HELP US TO ESTABLISH THE RIGHT PRIORITIES

We must prioritize. How we spend our time is a good indicator of where we have placed our priorities. Where we are dedicating our time is where we are dedicated. Is God's Word a priority? Is God's work a priority? Is God a priority?

Often what we call our priorities are only the things that ought to be our priorities, but they are not really getting the time to make them priorities. For example, someone may say, "My family is a priority." Maybe he is saying that because he knows it should be a priority, but it is not receiving the time it needs to be a priority.

David said, *"Is there not a cause?"* This helped him to prioritize his life. It helped him to keep his Lord in the place of preeminence.

> *Is the fire still burning, or are we just going through the motions?*

Keeping Christ in the place of preeminence provides properly placed priorities for all else in life.

The army of Israel needed feeding. They needed training. They needed equipping. Perhaps they needed some medical attention from the normal routine things that came up in military life. There were all kinds of things going on in that army camp, but there was nothing more important than the fact that someone needed to trust God for the faith to fight Goliath.

Many things are important, and some are very important; but only One is preeminent. The Lord Jesus Christ is never to be "one of"; He is the "One and only." David did not fight the giant because the giant needed to be defeated. He fought the giant because God must be obeyed.

HIS CAUSE DEMANDS A SACRIFICE

In I Samuel 17:31-32 the Bible says,

> *And when the words were heard which David spake, they rehearsed them before Saul: and he sent for him. And David said to Saul, Let no man's heart fail because of him; thy servant will go and fight with this Philistine.*

Obeying God costs something; it does not come easy or cheap. The entire camp was filled with soldiers, but one man said, "I will go. I will do it. I will fight him."

48

The work of God cannot be done with our spare resources. David was willing to put his life on the line. He took the greatest risk. This faith life became a part of the fabric of David's life.

In II Samuel 24, we see an event later in David's life that illustrates this so very well. David was about to buy a piece of ground on which to build a place to worship the Lord. He went to see a man named Araunah. The Bible says in verses twenty through twenty-four,

> *And Araunah looked, and saw the king and his servants coming on toward him: and Araunah went out, and bowed himself before the king on his face upon the ground. And Araunah said, Wherefore is my lord the king come to his servant? And David said, To buy the threshingloor of thee, to build an altar unto the LORD, that the plague may be stayed from the people. And Araunah said unto David, Let my lord the king take and offer up what seemeth good unto him: behold, here be oxen for burnt sacrifice, and threshing instruments and other instruments of the oxen for wood. All these things did Araunah, as a king, give unto the king. And Araunah said unto the king, The LORD thy God accept thee. And the king said unto Araunah, Nay; but I will surely buy it of thee at a price: neither will I offer burnt offerings unto the LORD my God of that which doth cost me nothing. So David bought the threshingfloor and the oxen for fifty shekels of silver.*

David said, *"Neither will I offer burnt offerings unto the LORD my God of that which doth cost me nothing."* God has designed the Christian life so that the people who yield, give, surrender, and sacrifice to God of themselves, receive the greatest blessing. The people who hold onto their lives and say, "Lord, it is mine; I will do with it as I please; I will make the decisions; I will yield only a part of it to You," get the least blessing and the least fulfillment. God has designed the Christian life so that as we give and yield our lives to Him, we receive the greatest blessing from the greatest yielding. When David said, *"Is there not a cause?"* he realized that it demanded a sacrifice.

HIS CAUSE REQUIRES MORE THAN THE ENERGY OF THE FLESH

The Bible says in I Samuel 17:45 that as David met the Philistine giant, he said to him, *"Thou comest to me with a sword, and with a spear, and with a shield: but I come to thee in the name of the LORD of hosts, the God of the armies of Israel, whom thou hast defied."*

David realized that it would take more than the energy of the flesh to do the work of God. Have you ever become weary in well doing? Do you realize that God has a purpose for weariness just as He has a purpose for strength? God has a purpose for difficulty as much as He has a purpose for deliverance. God has a purpose for trials as much as He has a purpose for triumph and victory. His strength is made perfect in our weakness (II Corinthians 12:9). As we become weaker and weaker, we must realize our need of His strength. God, in so many ways, allows us to see that we need Him. Again and again we come to know that His work requires His strength.

Most good people are sidetracked with good things. They trade a good thing for the best thing God has given us to do.

The giant came to David with everything a man could gather: a body nearly ten feet tall, weapons that most men could not even

carry, a sword and an armor bearer. Still these were no match for a shepherd boy clothed in the strength of the Lord.

The Bible says in I Samuel 17:45-46,

> *Then said David to the Philistine, Thou comest to me with a sword, and with a spear, and with a shield: but I come to thee in the name of the L*ORD *of hosts, the God of the armies of Israel, whom thou hast defied. This day will the L*ORD *deliver thee into mine hand; and I will smite thee, and take thine head from thee; and I will give the carcases of the host of the Philistines this day unto the fowls of the air, and to the wild beasts of the earth; that all the earth may know that there is a God in Israel.*

When we come to the place of yielding our lives to God's disposal, then God avails Himself to us.

HIS CAUSE IS ETERNAL

What David did that day was bigger than David. What I am doing as a Christian is more far reaching than my life. The cause in which I am involved is bigger than me, and greater than any one person. The work of God reaches much farther than my station, my place, or my time on earth. The grace of God has allowed me to have a part in something that is eternal. God placed me in the framework of time into something that takes in all eternity. The Bible says, *"The world passeth away, and the lust thereof: but he that doeth the will of God abideth for ever"* (I John 2:17).

This helps me not to become discouraged over one failure. It helps me not to get upset when we do not arrive at one particular goal when I planned that we would arrive at that one particular goal, because God's work is eternal. His calendar is not the same as mine.

The question is not if He is on my schedule, but am I on His? I am afraid that most of the time we try to put Him on our schedule. We attempt to squeeze Him in and say, "Lord, this is when it has to be done. This is when I want it, and this is the way I want it." God lets us get there, and we wonder, "Where is the Lord?" He is not working on our timetable. It is not necessarily that He does not want to, but He wants us to learn that we are to work on His.

> *How we spend our time is a good indicator of where we have placed our priorities.*

David said in verse forty-seven, *"And all this assembly shall know that the LORD saveth not with sword and spear: for the battle is the LORD's, and he will give you into our hands."* We have been given the glorious opportunity to touch eternity while we are here in time if we keep the cause of Christ before us. May God help us to do that.

CHAPTER FIVE

BY FORCE OR BY FAITH

hoose your weapons. How shall we live? Each one of us has already made a choice. Perhaps we do not even realize we have made the choice, but we have. We are either living by force or by faith.

The Bible says in I Samuel 17:45, *"Then said David to the Philistine, Thou comest to me with a sword, and with a spear, and with a shield: but I come to thee in the name of the LORD of hosts, the God of the armies of Israel, whom thou hast defied."*

David summarized the battle that was about to take place. It was not really a battle between a shepherd boy and a giant. It was not even a battle between the army of Israel and the army of the Philistines, though it may have appeared at first glance to be a national conflict represented by two champions, one representing each nation. David declared, *"Thou comest to me with a sword, and with a spear, and with a shield: but I come to thee in the name of the LORD of hosts."*

Notice how carefully God states this for us. Again we read, *"Then said David to the Philistine, Thou comest to me..."* This is the way the giant was coming, *"...with a sword, and with a spear, and with a shield..."* Then David said, *"...But I come to thee in the name of the* LORD *of hosts."*

I have both of these expressions circled in my Bible, *"thou comest to me"* and *"I come to thee."* I have a line drawn between them. It is always one way or the other; it is never both. We must decide whether we are going to face our problems with a spear, and with a sword, and with a shield, or if we are going to face them in the name of the Lord. We are all going to live either by force or by faith.

> *It is always one way or the other; it is never both. We must decide whether we are going to face our problems with a spear, and with a sword, and with a shield, or if we are going to face them in the name of the Lord. We are all going to live either by force or by faith.*

It goes without saying that the world's way is the force way. "I can overpower you. I can outrun you. I can out-scheme you. I can out-talk you. I can out-anger you. I can out-scream you. I can out-fight you. I can out-spend you. I can out-force you." That is the world's way. That is the only way those who do not know Christ operate. That is the world's way, whether it is in business, at home, or in personal conflict. It may manifest itself in many different forms, but it is always the same. It is not the Lord's way.

The Lord's way is to trust in Him. That is the faith way. There is one open secret that reveals whether we are living by force or by faith—our secret, private prayer life. No matter what we say about how we are living, we are not living the faith way if we do not have a prayer life. I hate to admit this because it convicts me; but it is true.

I was in Florida speaking and a young man came to see me about an important decision he was facing. We took a long walk together and stopped over a river bridge just to chat. He was a Christian, and as we talked, I spoke to him about his life. He said, "I am trying to decide how I am going to live." I said, "Explain your ideas to me." He said, "I am trying to decide if I am going to live by faith or not." He was honestly admitting the personal struggle that takes place in each of our lives.

Do you know that once you come to the place where you trust God, everything else is settled? The fact that Goliath was a soldier, a giant, and a Philistine champion did not have anything to do with whether David would go down into the valley or not. It was all dependent on whether or not David would trust God. Once David placed his faith in God, everything else was settled. I think we fight many battles  *We are either living by force or by faith.* we do not need to fight, and get involved in many skirmishes we do not need to be involved in. The truth is that we have one great thing to decide; it is whether or not we are going to trust God.

How are you going to live? In your personal life, family life, and business life, are you going to live by faith or by force?

There is only one way to know Jesus Christ. Do you know Him? You may have grown up in a Christian home and have a Christian mom and dad, but this does not make you a Christian. There is only one way to God. That is to know Him by personally trusting Him by faith as your Savior. Have you trusted Him?

This decision to live by faith cannot be made by anyone else. By faith, take every need in your life to the Lord. Many people are crushed under a weight God never intended for them to carry.

I Peter 5:7 says, *"Casting all your care upon him; for he careth for you."* Cast all your care upon the Lord Jesus.

THE FAITH LIFE HONORS GOD

The faith life honors God; the force life honors men. If you know the Lord Jesus as your Savior, that does not necessarily mean that you are living a faith life. It is possible to know the Lord as your Savior and still live by force. We will come back to our story, but first I would like for you to consider what we find in the book of I Corinthians as the apostle Paul is writing to the church in Corinth. We read in I Corinthians 3:1, *"And I, brethren, could not speak unto you as unto spiritual, but as unto carnal, even as unto babes in Christ."*

There is one open secret that reveals whether we are living by force or by faith–our secret, private prayer life.

In the first verse of the third chapter of I Corinthians, the apostle Paul says, "I am dealing with saved people. I am dealing with people who have asked the Lord to forgive their sin, and by faith received Christ as Savior." By the way, you need to make sure of that. You need to make sure that you have trusted Christ as your Savior. Paul said, "I am dealing with saved people, but some of you are not spiritual; you are carnal."

Let us consider again I Samuel 17. The Philistines had decided how this battle was going to be fought. It was going to be a force issue. They held all of Israel at bay by determining how it was going to be done. They said, "We are going to choose the biggest, strongest, roughest, toughest guy and you choose the biggest, strongest, roughest, toughest guy, and we are going to let the biggest, strongest, roughest, toughest guys have it out. The one who wins takes all."

They determined the rules. It did not sound that bad until the giant stepped out. Israel could not match that force.

To make bad matters worse, Saul had taken on this Philistine philosophy. He lived a life of force. He thought everyone must be overpowered. If the victory was going to be won, it had to be won matching force against force. This is how it had to be fought, on Philistine terms.

Do you realize what most people have allowed the world to do? They have allowed the world to determine how they are going to live their lives. They have allowed the world to set the bounds and make the rules. Remember, friend, we are in the world, but not of the world. The Christian, by the grace of God, is to live a faith life in a world of force.

Sadly, many of us use the same foolish tactics the world uses. However, God's Word tells us the weapons of our warfare are not the weapons of our enemies. Our God is almighty and He has given us weapons that can only be appropriated by faith.

THE FAITH LIFE IS RARELY FOUND

As Goliath continued his threats, the search was on in Israel's camp. They were looking for a man who would go down into the valley and face Goliath. No one could be found. It is not always easy to find someone who lives by faith.

To all of our shame, we spend so little time with God. We place greater value on lesser things. Most of us take more time getting ourselves dressed than we do praying. We must redeem the time, because the days are evil. I am not sounding an alarm; the alarm has been sounding for years. The Christian life is the faith life.

The reason the entire army of Israel would not move was because they had learned to live by force, not by faith. The reason there is so little advance in God's work is that we have lost sight of the greatness of God. We feel overpowered, and we wonder what we can do. By faith, we must move forward, press on, and claim the victory.

THE FAITH LIFE PROTECTS

Look again at this conversation. The Bible says in I Samuel 17:45, *"Thou comest to me with a sword, and with a spear, and with a shield: but I come to thee in the name of the LORD."*

The big guy with all the weapons felt protected. However, it was the fellow who walked down into the valley in the strength of the Lord who was really protected. Do you know that apart from God there is no protection, but in the center of God's will, there is safety? If God calls you to the most primitive place among cruel people to

The Christian life is the faith life.

serve Him, if that is the center of God's will for your life, it is safer than sitting under a shade tree in a quaint country town. The faith life protects us. The force life endangers us.

The Word of God declares to us that David won that victory. As David took pen in hand and the Spirit of God gave him the words to write, he said in Psalm 34:1-7,

> *I will bless the LORD at all times: his praise shall continually be in my mouth. My soul shall make her boast in the LORD: the humble shall hear thereof, and be glad. O magnify the LORD with me, and let us exalt his name together. I sought the LORD, and he heard me, and delivered me from all my fears. They looked unto him, and were lightened: and their faces were not ashamed. This poor man cried, and the LORD heard him, and saved him out of all his troubles. The*

angel of the LORD encampeth round about them that fear him, and delivereth them.

The angel of the Lord is round about them that fear him. We are trusting God, believing Him, leaning on Him, and fearing Him. God says His angels are encamped *"round about them that fear him."* Do you know that wherever we go, whatever we do in the name of the Lord, whatever we attempt to do by God's grace in faith, the Lord promises to be with us? Though He indwells us and will never leave or forsake us as Christians, if we live by force, God will allow us to fail.

There is a difference between the faith life and the force life. We throw ourselves open to every enemy when we try to live by force; but our God protects us and encamps round about us when we live by faith.

There is no way under heaven that I can completely protect myself from people. Any man, any woman, anywhere, anytime, can say anything they please. Many have said things they should never have said, and the Lord will reward them according to their deeds. Our God will protect His children. Paul said of Alexander the coppersmith, *"The Lord reward him according to his works"* (II Timothy 4:14).

David had nothing to worry about. The truth is, the giant had everything to be alarmed about because force endangers, but faith in God protects.

THE VICTORY OF THE FAITH LIFE IS ETERNAL

Notice what the Bible says, *"Thou comest to me with a sword, and with a spear, and with a shield: but I come to thee in the name of the LORD of hosts, the God of the armies of Israel, whom thou hast defied."*

God gave David a victory that day that was long lasting. It affected the entire nation. Never forget that we are going to reap what we have sown, and we are reaping today what has already been sown in the past. Here is the secret–David did not decide on the day he fought Goliath that he was going to live by faith; he made that decision long before he ever faced Goliath. It was a vital part of his life. David did not start living by faith the day he killed Goliath. He said plainly to Saul, *"The Lord...delivered me out of the paw of the lion, and out of the paw of the bear."* He had already learned to live by faith. Though faith must always be in the present tense, the faith life encourages us to continue to live by faith.

> *Though faith must always be in the present tense, the faith life encourages us to continue to live by faith.*

It is not simply a matter of "faith action" that we need; it is a "faith life" that we need. We cannot continue to live the force life and expect God's blessing. You may have one short-term victory after another. You may have won an argument or a fight, but you will face the very same battle again tomorrow. The Christian life requires faith each day, but determining to live the faith life and doing God's will abides forever.

David was a giant-killer, but more than a giant-killer, he was a man of faith in God. The Bible says in verse forty-six, *"This day will the Lord deliver thee into mine hand; and I will smite thee, and take thine head from thee; and I will give the carcases of the host of the Philistines this day unto the fowls of the air, and to the wild beasts of the earth; that all the earth may know that there is a God in Israel."*

He does not say that everyone will know that David is the heavyweight champion of Israel. He says, *"That all the earth may know that there is a God in Israel."*

The faith life honors God. The force life honors man. It is not whether I am right or wrong that matters. It is whether God is glorified or not that matters. In my home, it is not whether I am the boss or not that matters. God gave me the responsibility of being the head of the home by the fact that I am a man. It is whether the Lord Jesus is glorified in my home or not that matters. Do my children see the Lord in their father's life? This is what really matters. This is the difference between living life by faith and living life by force.

CHAPTER SIX

DAVID RETURNED

aith in God takes us into the great conflicts of life, and His promises see us through. In I Samuel 17, David had dedicated himself to God in the private secret place of his heart and was ready to be used of God on this particular occasion. He walked down the slope of the hillside and faced Goliath. He did battle with that giant and cut off his head. He lifted up the head as a testimony of God's power and shook the head of Goliath in the face of the Philistines. Like little dogs with their tails between their legs, the Philistines ran in fear all the way to the Mediterranean Sea as the army of Israel chased them.

The Bible says in I Samuel 17:57-58, *"And as David returned from the slaughter of the Philistine, Abner took him, and brought him before Saul with the head of the Philistine in his hand. And Saul said to him, Whose son art thou, thou young man? And David answered, I am the son of thy servant Jesse the Bethlehemite."* David returned!

If we had been a part of the army of Israel and had seen David going down to face Goliath, we most likely would have been saying something like this, "There is no way he can face that giant and ever come back alive. He will never make it. It just cannot be done."

In Philippians 4:13 the Bible says, *"I can do all things through Christ which strengtheneth me."* We must remember that we can do all things through Christ.

THE LORD DELIVERED DAVID

The Lord delivered him. That is exactly what David said God would do. If you will notice in verses forty-five and forty-six, where David made his speech to Goliath, the Bible says, *"Then said David to the Philistine, Thou comest to me with a sword, and with a spear, and with a shield: but I come to thee in the name of the LORD of hosts, the God of the armies of Israel, whom thou hast defied. This day will the LORD deliver thee into mine hand."*

David said, *"This day the LORD will deliver thee into mine hand."* After the battle when David came carrying the head of the Philistine giant right into the presence of Saul, Saul said, "Whose son are you?" David had already been in the king's court playing his harp, but Saul had made a promise that anyone who killed the giant would be rewarded. Part of his reward was that his father's house would be free in Israel, so the king had to find out about David's father. Maybe he knew and had forgotten. David said boldly, "I am the son of Jesse from Bethlehem."

No doubt David had developed into a young man and his appearance which had been boyish was much more like a man. There is a certain time when the boyishness leaves and the boy looks much more like a man. I imagine this is what had happened to David since Saul had last seen him.

As David carried the head of that Philistine, no doubt with fresh blood still dripping from it, into the presence of the cowardly King Saul, there was a testimony given without saying a single word. The Lord delivered him. Actions speak more loudly than words.

When David came into the tent of King Saul carrying the head of that Philistine giant in his hand, it was a sight never to be forgotten. It was a testimony that the Lord does deliver His people, that He brings them through.

In that moment we have a portrait of two totally different men. Saul had such a promising start and such a tragic ending; David came from the sheepfold to the throne.

David went down into the valley, faced the giant, and came back alive. The victory in David's life was a sure sign of defeat in Saul's. After that battle, both men would never be the same.

There is a beautiful promise in the book of Philippians that I want you to remember. The Bible says in Philippians 1:6, *"Being confident of this very thing, that he which hath begun a good work in you will perform it until the day of Jesus Christ."*

God will finish His work! We need to be very sure that we know God has started working. What has He started in you? Have you asked the Lord to forgive your sin and by faith received Jesus Christ as your Savior?

THE LAND WAS BLESSED BECAUSE OF DAVID'S RETURN

We learn from this story that what we do or refuse to do has an effect on other people. How we live or refuse to live has an effect on others. The Bible says in I Samuel 17:46-47,

> *This day will the LORD deliver thee into mine*
> *hand; and I will smite thee, and take thine head from*
> *thee; and I will give the carcases of the host of the*
> *Philistines this day unto the fowls of the air, and to the*
> *wild beasts of the earth; that all the earth may know*
> *that there is a God in Israel. And all this assembly*
> *shall know that the LORD saveth not with sword and*
> *spear: for the battle is the LORD's, and he will give*
> *you into our hands.*

David knew that what he did had an effect on all Israel. The land was blessed; the people were rewarded. All Israelites were encouraged by David's faith in God. I never cease to be amazed at what the Lord can do through the life of one person to bless millions of people.

You can sin and every one in your home is affected by it. There are things you could do that would influence your children adversely for the rest of their lives. I could do something that my wife and two sons would be affected by and would carry in their hearts and minds the rest of their lives. If we can cause that much harm by evil, think how much good we can cause by doing right and obeying God.

Most of the time we magnify the evil by talking about the evil things people have done; but David did the right thing, and the entire nation was blessed by it. What a responsibility we have to do what God says! When we return, there is a song of victory; it is a time of praise. God is honored, and people are blessed. God is thanked. *"The battle is the LORD's."*

Husbands, you can be an encouragement to your wives if you will follow the Lord. Simply by the way you live with faith in God, you can encourage her. Wives, you can be an encouragement to your husbands if you live with faith in God. Parents, you can be a help to your children if you live with faith in God. Children, you can be a help to your parents if you live with faith in God. Every little grandson and granddaughter needs a granddaddy and a grandmother who has faith in God. Children who know the Lord like to think that their family members love God and live right.

The land was blessed when David returned. He stood before King Saul, with Abner standing by his side, and Goliath's head in his hand. Gathered outside of Saul's tent was an entire army. They were people who had lost all courage and hope, who believed that they were in some pitiful bondage from which they would never escape. One man's deed aroused a nation to believe God.

As David carried the head of that Philistine, no doubt with fresh blood still dripping from it, into the presence of the cowardly King Saul, there was a testimony given without saying a single word.

By the way we live we can change a workplace; we can make God known. By the way we live we can change a home; we can make God known. By the way we live we can revive a Sunday School class; we can make God known. Someone you work with, someone who lives under the same roof with you, someone you know who looks at you every day will be affected for good, and for God, and for eternity if you demonstrate faith in the Lord.

In Proverbs chapter thirty-one, the Bible says that the children of a godly mother rise up and call her blessed. Why? Because she honors God with her life, living for the Lord, and honoring her family. If your children had to say today what they think of your Christianity, what would they say?

Fathers, this is not simply a matter of taking care of them and providing for them. It is a mistake to think that we have done for our children what we should if all we can say is, "They eat well. They have nice clothes to wear. They have a fine house in which to live." Do they have a father who walks with God? Your children would be better off to go to the "second-hand store" to get their clothes, and have a Christian daddy who honors God, than to live in the nicest house in your city, and have a father who does not honor God.

> *We have a portrait of two totally different men. Saul had such a promising start and such a tragic ending; David came from the sheepfold to the throne.*

People who know the Lord Jesus need to live so that others can see Christ in them. If you had taken a survey among those men in Saul's army and asked, "How many of you believe there is a God in heaven?" they would all have raised their hands. If you asked, "How many of you believe that God is bigger than that giant?" they would all have raised their hands. If you had asked, "How many of you will believe God to help you and enable you to go down there and deal with that giant?" none would have volunteered. Only one man did that.

The Christian life is more than nodding our heads in agreement in church. It is trusting God for daily strength and seeing our God prove Himself to us. As we trust Him, we find the victory we need.

Many people retire on God. At what age are you going to retire on the Lord? Are you going to retire just about the time your grandchildren need to know that you are a Christian? Are you going to retire about the time one of your children gets married and needs your godly example in marriage? Are you going to retire on God about the time you are getting ready to die, and people will have to go to a graveside with questions concerning your faith?

The Lord delivered David and the land was blessed because David put his faith in God. May the Lord convict us to dedicate ourselves to our God and the task at hand.

THE LIFE OF DAVID WAS CHANGED FOREVER

David's life would never be the same. As we look for the miraculous to take place, the Lord takes the ordinary and touches it in a miraculous way.

When David started out the day before, he was singing to the sheep. Now the entire nation is singing about David. He started out the day before, and no one knew who he was; now he is a national hero. In one sense, he became a captive of his fame. Greater things were expected of him, and rightly so, than were expected the day before.

God raises up men and gives them visibility. The Lord does these things and expects us to live accountable lives. This we understand, but that is not how his life was changed.

The way I am thinking about his life being changed is that God did something for David that he could never forget. As long as he lived, he would remember that God delivered that giant. He could not get away from it.

There are things too personal for me to share with you, things that God has done for me that I will never forget. God broke through and answered prayer. He stopped things that every one had planned that "could not" be stopped. The Lord has proven to me in deeply personal ways that He is real.

Once David went down into that valley and God proved Himself to David by killing that giant, David's life was never the same. The point is that in those hours of trial and deliverance, many of us have said to God, "Lord, I promise You that from this day forward, I will be different. I will be faithful. I will never break Your heart again." Many of us in those experiences have made promises to God. It may have been by a hospital bed, in a near family breakup, or in some other moment of need that promises were made. We made promises to God that we have allowed to grow cold in our hearts. Now, He reminds us of His goodness.

> *As we look for the miraculous to take place, the Lord takes the ordinary and touches it in a miraculous way.*

We need to say, "Lord, the same zeal and love I had for You when You delivered me then, I want again." The Bible says, *"David returned"* from the slaughter of this Philistine. God brought him back.

God will bring you through. The Lord delivers when we trust Him, and those about us are blessed because of it. Our lives are changed forever as God proves Himself to us.

CHAPTER SEVEN

DAVID AND JONATHAN

riendship is one of God's special gifts to the human race. Stop and thank the Lord for your friends. More importantly, ask the Lord to help you be a true friend.

In the eighteenth chapter of the book of I Samuel, we come across two names. The Bible is filled with names, and some seem to go together so well. None go together any better than do the names of David and Jonathan.

The Bible says in I Samuel 18:1-4,

> *And it came to pass, when he had made an end of speaking unto Saul, that the soul of Jonathan was knit with the soul of David, and Jonathan loved him as his own soul. And Saul took him that day, and would let him go no more home to his father's house. Then Jonathan and David made a covenant, because he loved him as his own soul. And Jonathan stripped himself of the robe that was upon him, and gave it to*

David and Jonathan

David, and his garments, even to his sword, and to his bow, and to his girdle.

Note well the names of these two men, David and Jonathan. David had done battle with Goliath. One of the tremendous tests in his life had passed, and he had come out at the head of the class. He trusted the Lord completely and the Lord gave the victory.

> *Something was looming much larger in David's life. It would be more severe than any Goliath David would ever have to face. He would have to deal with the rage and jealousy of King Saul.*

Something was looming much larger in David's life. It would be more severe than any Goliath David would ever have to face. He would have to deal with the rage and jealousy of King Saul.

So often in life, we think we have passed the test only to find that it was simply the first in a series. God has a way of building His children, by having us deal with severity in degrees and learn to trust Him day by day.

As great a test as it was for David to face Goliath, it was not nearly the test that facing Saul proved to be. It is most interesting and helpful to find out what God did to help David deal with Saul.

Saul was the king who tried to kill David. Saul became filled with rage and jealousy. His anger was out of control. God spared the life of David in such a way that the only way it could have been explained was that God did it. On one occasion, Saul took his spear in hand, and with steady aim, threw it at David. He was a trained soldier who could have killed any moving animal, much less a man standing there; but God spared David.

How was God going to help David deal with such a man as Saul? The answer was very simple. He gave David a friend.

Many men and women have faced a seemingly insurmountable trial in life, and God gave them a friend to help them through. Many a man has thought, "I will never get another job. I cannot support my family. I am finished. My life is ruined and wrecked. It is all gone." Then God gave him a friend.

In the morning of the battle with Goliath, David's eldest brother Eliab turned from him, but in the evening God gave David the heart of Jonathan, a friend that proved to stick closer than a brother. Many men have thought they could not finish the task, but God gave them a friend. Many pastors have thought the task was too great, but God gave them a friend.

The Lord has been good to me this way. I am thinking of one particular man now who came to my aid with his friendship in a period of severe testing and trial. He is now in heaven; but oh, what a friend he was to me.

God gave David a friend. You might think it interesting to note that Jonathan was more than likely twice David's age. David, in age, would have been more of a son than a bosom buddy. However, Jonathan became his friend.

> *How was God going to help David deal with such a man as Saul? The answer was very simple. He gave David a friend.*

I grew up in the beautiful little southern town of Maryville, Tennessee, and went to Everett High School. My wife and I graduated from high school together. At that school I had an outstanding Christian principal who took a keen interest in me. Mr. Davis said to me on one occasion, "Clarence, when you go through life, if you count a handful of people as your true friends, you are a very wealthy man." That was many years ago, and I am understanding more fully day by day what that kind man meant when he said "true friends."

God wants every one of us to be a friend. This is the Lord's desire. God gave David a friend; his name was Jonathan.

THE ENTERING INTO THIS FRIENDSHIP

The Bible says in verse one, *"And it came to pass, when he had made an end of speaking unto Saul, that the soul of Jonathan was knit with the soul of David, and Jonathan loved him as his own soul."*

God uses the word *"knit"* to show us that their souls were bound together, or sewn together. They entered into a friendship. Jonathan had already proven himself as a courageous soldier. He was every inch a man! We learn this fact earlier in the accounts of the Word of God.

Jonathan was by his father's side when David went forth to meet Goliath. Jonathan loved his father and had been steadfast with him. When David returned from fighting Goliath with Goliath's head in his hand, Jonathan was standing by his father's side. He listened to the comments that Saul made to David. As he listened, his soul was knit with David and they entered into a friendship.

One would think this friendship was strange if you tried to bring these two together on any other terms. One was a prince and the other a poor shepherd. As a matter of fact, Jonathan was the crown prince. He was the oldest of the sons of Saul, the rightful heir to the throne of Israel. He was Crown Prince Jonathan. He was much older than David.

David was just an ordinary fellow. He grew up in Bethlehem as a shepherd boy. On this day, the crown prince of Israel had his soul knit together with the shepherd boy. David would someday be the king of Israel, not Jonathan.

Search your mind and recall who your true friends are. How did you form those friendships? The Bible says in Proverbs 22:1, *"A good name is rather to be chosen than great riches, and loving favour rather than silver and gold."*

Remember the expression, *"loving favour rather than silver and gold."* God did something in Jonathan's heart as he was standing by his father beholding this young warrior. God caused David to have favor in the heart of Jonathan. Jonathan's heart was joined to David's, and they entered into this friendship. Did you know that in the providential care of God in our lives, He allows us to come in contact with people? He allows people to walk into our offices, to come into our homes, and to enter into our lives. He means for us to befriend them and to be a help to them.

No one could have imagined on that day when David became a national hero and the headless giant's body lay in the valley of Elah, that David would have needed such a friend.

Did you ever think that God sent someone to you who needed a friend? No one could have imagined on that day when David became a national hero and the headless giant's body lay in the valley of Elah, that David would have needed such a friend. But God knew that King Saul would be the enemy of David and that David would need such a friend.

We do not know what is down the road. We do not know what is around the corner; but God has done something in the human heart that allows us to befriend one another. We need to enter into those friendships that are pure and wholesome and honoring to God.

You can find selfish people all over the world. Do you know how you spot them? They are alone. Perhaps you can find exceptions to this, but remember the truth of the Word of God in Proverbs 18:24, *"A man that hath friends must shew himself friendly: and there is a friend that sticketh closer than a brother."*

THE EXPRESSION
OF THIS FRIENDSHIP

This friendship was not self-serving; it was self-sacrificing. Humanly speaking, there was nothing Jonathan could gain from David. There was nothing David had in his possession that he could have given to Jonathan, but Jonathan befriended him. Notice carefully how Jonathan expressed this friendship. The Bible says in I Samuel 18:2-4,

> *And Saul took him that day, and would let him go no more home to his father's house. Then Jonathan and David made a covenant, because he loved him as his own soul. And Jonathan stripped himself of the robe that was upon him, and gave it to David, and his garments, even to his sword, and to his bow, and to his girdle.*

David stood in the tent with Saul and Saul said, "You can't go home to your father." Jonathan went to David and did a most amazing thing. He gave David his sword, his bow, and his other weapons. By his action Jonathan declared to David, "I am expressing my soul to you. I am saying to you that the way you live by faith in God, trusting God, facing the giant, and leaning on God for strength is the right way. It is not by force, by sword, by spear, by royalty, or by heritage; it is by faith in God. I want your way. I believe in your way. I want to live your way."

By placing his royal robe on David, he was declaring, "I love God, and I love Israel. You, David, can be king in my place."

Can you imagine a human heart so full of love for God and a man that he would say, "You can be the king. I am the crown prince, but you can be the king"? No wonder this example of David and Jonathan is lifted up to us as such a model of friendship and devotion. More than that, Jonathan humbled himself before this shepherd boy and by his actions said, "My father's way and the way we have chosen, the way of force, is not the right way. The faith way is the right way."

The Bible says that they entered into a covenant together. I have done some interesting reading on this particular covenant and how they may have shared this covenant. It may have been with an exchange of things, with blood, and with certain gestures and handshakes with their own blood on their hands. They may have joined their arms together. Nevertheless, the Bible says they entered into a covenant.

The thing God wants us to see is that when they exchanged garments, when Saul's son Jonathan gave David his robe, he was saying, "There is one right way to live, and you are living that way. I acknowledge that your way is the right way. This is what I want for my life and I surrender to you my right to the throne."

We find an example of that in the life of Peter. In the fifth chapter of Luke, Peter had been out all night fishing. He had been trying all night to catch fish, but had caught nothing. The Lord Jesus said, "Launch out into the deep for a great draught of fish."

When Peter launched out into the deep, he found that his net was so full the boats were about to sink. As soon as he got back to the shore, Peter fell at Jesus' knees saying, *"Depart from me; for I am a sinful man, O Lord."*

Peter said, "Lord, I have tried my way. I have tried to do it my way, but I want You to know that I believe Your way is the right way." He fell at the feet of the Lord Jesus and said, "I give myself to You."

God has something for us to learn in this. There is a specific purpose for God recording the entering into and the expression of the friendship between David and Jonathan and the way Jonathan behaved himself.

God wants us to see that the way David lived is the way we should live. Faithing God and glorifying God is the way of the believer.

THE EXAMPLE OF THIS FRIENDSHIP

It has been three thousand years since this event took place after the battle with Goliath, and I am writing about it. The influence of their example is far-reaching; it is eternal.

David learned that God was in every step he took. He did not know on the day he defeated Goliath how important it would be to have such a friend as Jonathan, but he soon learned. The example of this friendship should stir our hearts.

I wish I could be a little more personal than I am able to be. The only reason I feel an inability is for fear of embarrassing people. There are people I love who would be gone, their lives completely wasted, had not the Lord given someone to befriend and help them.

Do you know that you and I have the power and responsibility from the Lord to encourage people? We exercise much of that power over our own children; but we can do something for people by being a true Christian friend to them that almost no one else can do.

Someone once called me with a message that was not true concerning one of my friends. I called my friend and said, "This is what was said last evening. I want you to know it is a lie. I want you to know that you are my friend, and I believe I am your friend. I don't want the Devil to come between our friendship." That was important to me, and I believe it was important to my friend.

I learned something about that kind of loyalty from an example friendship like Jonathan had with David. There is even more to it than this though. The Bible says, *"There is a friend that sticketh closer than a brother"* (Proverbs 18:24).

In the fifteenth chapter of the Gospel according to Luke, the Bible records that publicans and sinners gathered with the Lord Jesus. When the scribes and Pharisees saw this they said, "Look at Him! He is a friend of publicans and sinners."

Our Lord Jesus knew what they were saying, and He began to tell the story of a man who had one hundred sheep, and one of them was lost. He loved that lost sheep so much that he risked his life to save it. He told them also of a woman who had ten precious coins, and the loss of one of them meant it must be found. She searched the house until she found it. He spoke of a father who had two sons, and one of them left home, but he never gave up on him.

The Lord Jesus let them know that He was not only a friend; He was willing to come to earth to find them. He was willing to go to Calvary to save them. He was willing to seek and to suffer until they were found.

I have a Friend whose name is Jesus Christ. He has forgiven my sin and saved my soul. He has given me a home in heaven. He has changed my life. He has done all of this and so much more for me, and I have deserved none of it. Because of what He has done for me, I want to be a friend to others. I serve the Lord because of what He has done for me.

Chapter Eight

The Behavior of a Hero

ne way to gain insight into the lives of people is to look at their heroes. As a matter of fact, one way to study history is to study it by looking at the prominent figures in history. In the end, the people we admire are the people to whom we give our allegiance.

In the eighteenth chapter of the book of I Samuel, we find a hero and we learn that fame is much more difficult to deal with than failure. Fame has ruined more people than failure.

Notice carefully what we find in I Samuel 18. Let us look at what happened to David after he killed the giant. The Bible says in verses five through fifteen,

> *And David went out whithersoever Saul sent him, and behaved himself wisely: and Saul set him over the men of war, and he was accepted in the sight of all the people, and also in the sight of Saul's servants. And it came to pass as they came, when David was*

returned from the slaughter of the Philistine, that the women came out of all cities of Israel, singing and dancing, to meet king Saul, with tabrets, with joy, and with instruments of musick. And the women answered one another as they played, and said, Saul hath slain his thousands, and David his ten thousands. And Saul was very wroth, and the saying displeased him; and he said, They have ascribed unto David ten thousands, and to me they have ascribed but thousands: and what can he have more but the kingdom? And Saul eyed David from that day and forward. And it came to pass on the morrow, that the evil spirit from God came upon Saul, and he prophesied in the midst of the house: and David played with his hand, as at other times: and there was a javelin in Saul's hand. And Saul cast the javelin; for he said, I will smite David even to the wall with it. And David avoided out of his presence twice. And Saul was afraid of David, because the Lord was with him, and was departed from Saul. Therefore Saul removed him from him, and made him his captain over a thousand; and he went out and came in before the people. And David behaved himself wisely in all his ways; and the Lord was with him. Wherefore when Saul saw that he behaved himself very wisely, he was afraid of him.

One of the ways God speaks to us is by repetition. In these few verses of Scripture, God repeats something three times. He says in verse five that David *"behaved himself wisely."* He says in verse fourteen that *"David behaved himself wisely."* In verse fifteen, God says that David *"behaved himself very wisely."*

I have noticed all of my life and ministry that you can tell much about people when one of two things happens to them. First, when they are rebuked or reproved, their real character comes through. Second, when they are given authority. We find what is truly in people's hearts when they have been reproved or when they are given authority. In the eighteenth chapter of I Samuel, David is given authority, and the Bible says again and again that he behaved himself wisely.

Many times we say that we are Christians, but we do not behave like Christians. If you asked me, "Are you a Christian, Clarence Sexton?" I would answer, "Yes, I know I am Christian." I would give my testimony. I would tell you about when I asked God to forgive my sin and trusted Jesus Christ as my Savior. I would tell you of God's care and keeping of my life. But if you asked me, "Have you always behaved like a Christian?" I would be ashamed, but I would say to you, "Not always." I regret that. How about you?

We learn that fame is much more difficult to deal with than failure. Fame has ruined more people than failure.

God says that David behaved himself wisely. Anytime you see the word *wise* attributed to someone's behavior, it does not have to do primarily with his relationship with people, but with his relationship with God. The Bible says in Proverbs 9:10, *"The fear of the LORD is the beginning of wisdom."*

Every time God mentioned David's behavior, He said David behaved himself wisely. When He connected wise living with David's living, He was saying that David feared God. We do not behave wisely without putting God in the proper place in our lives. We behave a certain way because we believe a certain way. When we see anyone behave unwisely, it means that God is not given the proper place in that person's life. When God's Word says that David behaved himself wisely, it means that he recognized God's rightful place in his life, because wisdom and wise living comes from fearing the Lord.

If an individual puts God in the proper place, that individual is going to do right in his life. He is going to tell the truth on the job. He is going to keep a clean heart and a clean mouth if he fears God. We must not overlook this important truth. The reason David behaved himself wisely is that David feared the Lord in his private life.

> *We behave a certain way because we believe a certain way. When we see anyone behave unwisely, it means that God is not given the proper place in that person's life.*

One of the things we must always work with is our attitude. No one else exercises control over my attitude. They may exercise some influence over my attitude, but no one else exercises control over my attitude except me. I must constantly guard my attitude toward people, toward the ministry, toward what God has done for me, with me, and to me. I must guard my attitude and keep my attitude right.

Another thing that is always operative in our lives is our adversary. The Bible says in I Peter 5:8, *"Be sober, be vigilant; because your adversary the devil, as a roaring lion, walketh about, seeking whom he may devour."* We have an adversary, the Devil. God's Word says that we wrestle not against flesh and blood. When we have blow-ups, and flare-ups, and mess-ups, and crash-ups, who is behind all of it? It is our adversary.

As believers, the third thing that is always operative in our lives is our advocate. This is a Bible word. The Bible says in I John 2:1-2,

> *My little children these things write I unto you, that ye sin not. And if any man sin, we have an advocate with the Father, Jesus Christ the righteous: and he is*

the propitiation for our sins: and not for ours only,
but also for the sins of the whole world.

God says we have an advocate. That means that someone is pleading our case. He is taking things on our behalf to God the Father. The moment we sin, Christ pleads our case. We are not in this world alone.

We have an advocate if we are Christians. He is pleading our case. He is on our side. He is helping us; therefore, we must guard our attitude. We must be warned about our adversary. We must thank God for our advocate. All these things have to do with our behavior.

A man behaves a certain way because he believes a certain way. If a fellow does not believe in heaven or hell, he is going to live for this life only. He behaves a certain way because he believes a certain way. Our beliefs affect our behavior.

David behaved himself wisely because he believed a certain way. If we could bring people to this one thing, and we could bring ourselves to this one thing, that we must every day walk before God, it would change our lives. God hears us, sees us, and knows our thoughts. God knows all about us. David lived believing this to be true. As a result, he behaved wisely. Notice how David responded to people in this passage.

HIS BEHAVIOR AMONG HIS FELLOW SERVANTS

The Bible says in verse five of I Samuel 18,

And David went out whithersoever Saul sent him,
and behaved himself wisely: and Saul set him over

*the men of war, and he was accepted in the sight of all
the people, and also in the sight of Saul's servants.*

The Bible says he behaved wisely in the sight of Saul's servants.
There are not many people who can exercise the kind of leadership
that David exercised, and receive the type of recognition that David
did, and still have the deep gratitude and
appreciation of those who serve under
him. But David behaved himself wisely,
and he dealt with his fellow workers in a
way that honored God.

> *Success has
> caused many
> more casualties
> than failure.*

It does not make any difference what
title you hold on your job; you and I are
no better than those without titles. The
moment we think we are, we have lost God's honor on our lives. Of
course there is an order in authority and submission to authority in the
home, on the job, and in the church; but many people are dealing with
the temptation to think that the whole world revolves around them.

If you have one child in the school classroom who thinks it is his
classroom and the only thing that matters is what he wants, the entire
class will be disrupted by it. If you have one person in the church
who says, "This is my church and things are going to be done my
way. I am going to have it my way or no way," the entire church is
affected by it. David was not that kind of man. Why was he not that
kind of man? Because he put God in the proper place in his life, and
he dealt with his fellow workers with wisdom.

HIS BEHAVIOR AND HIS FAME

David killed the giant. The Bible says in verse six, *"And it came to
pass as they came, when David was returned from the slaughter of*

the Philistine..." They were thinking about one thing, the big giant. He was famous, and he had to deal with success and fame.

My wife and I were in a rather large Bible conference, and she was listening as I was speaking. We returned to the motel room, and she said to me, "I saw the people for an hour or so after the service gather around you to have you sign their Bibles and talk to them. They told you how they adored you and cared for you, but I want to tell you something–if you ever start thinking about yourself the way those people do about you, you are ruined." That was a great thing for me to hear.

If I ever think I am too good to pick up the paper towels that have been thrown aside on the bathroom floor, or to wipe out the sinks that are dirty, or to help the men unload the trucks, or to take care of anything that needs cared for, then I am in trouble. You may say, "But that's not your job." It may not be my job, but the people I love are involved in that job, and I should never think I am too good to help them do it. Success has caused many more casualties than failure.

We are all just sinners saved by the grace of God. You may manage a business, but you are no better than the people you manage. They have families. They have children. They have concerns. They have needs just as you have. May God help us to realize what kind of world we live in, a world of hurt and a world of great need. I like the behavior of this hero because he dealt with fame wisely.

HIS BEHAVIOR WITH THE FOOLISH KING

Notice that Saul listened as they sang returning from the slaughter of the Philistines. The women came out and they answered one another. They were singing and dancing. The Bible says, *"The women came out of all cities of Israel, singing and dancing, to meet king Saul, with tabrets, with joy, and with instruments of musick. And the women answered one another as they played, and said, Saul hath slain his thousands, and David his ten thousands."*

Saul listened, and he gave place to the Devil in his life. Do you know the Devil has set many of us up to hear something so that he can get a place in our lives? Ephesians 4:27 says, *"Neither give place to the devil."*

Saul gave place to the Devil. He listened; he lingered. Their words echoed in his mind. He said, "They are bragging on David and not on me." It took over in his life. The Bible says,

> *And Saul was very wroth, and the saying displeased him; and he said, They have ascribed unto David ten thousands, and to me they have ascribed but thousands: and what can he have more but the kingdom? And Saul eyed David from that day and forward. And it came to pass on the morrow, that the evil spirit from God came upon Saul...*

This does not mean that God is an evil spirit. It means that God is in charge of the whole universe, and God allowed an evil spirit to come to Saul.

The verse continues, saying of Saul, *"...and he prophesied."* As the Bible says in I John 4:1, we must try the spirits because it could be an evil spirit that is speaking through someone.

Saul had a javelin by his side. He was a man of war, and he said, "I am going to kill David right now." How many times, in a fit of anger, in a low moment, have we said or done something that we wished to God only moments later we had never said or done?

Saul twice took the javelin and tried to pin David's body to the wall; but God delivered David. When Saul saw God deliver him, he shook with fear because he knew that the only way he could have missed him was for God to have spared him. David could have grabbed the javelin and thrown it back at the king, but he did not. He behaved himself wisely.

In our natural hearts, we have the desire to get even with people. It is worse in some people than in others, but it is in all of us. If they hurt us, we want to hurt them. If they talk about us, we talk about them. If they get us, we are going to get them before they get us again. We must deal with this in life. Do you know why we have it to deal with? Because we are all a part of this fallen human race.

You have it to deal with in your home. Your wife may say something, and before long you have said something worse back to her. She says it back to you, and you say it back to her. Before long, you have trouble on your hands that could have been avoided if one of you had behaved as a Christian.

Look at churches where people fight and fuss. They all say they are believers, but they do not behave as Christians. Do you know why people who say they are Christians do not behave as Christians? It is because they do not give God the proper place in their lives.

Do you know the Devil has set many of us up to hear something so that he can get a place in our lives? Ephesians 4:27 says, "Neither give place to the devil."

David behaved himself wisely. The king tried to kill him, and David responded wisely. Later, David must deal with his own son. Later, David must deal with his own sin. All of us are dealing with someone or something that is difficult. Are we dealing with it wisely? Are we committing it to Jesus Christ?

Would you agree with me that so much heartache and trouble could be avoided if we would behave as Christians? Then all of us need to find our place before God. If there is someone we need to pray for, let us pray for that person. If there is someone we are fighting with, let us pray for him. All of us need to find our place before God and ask God to help us behave ourselves wisely. We need to take whatever it is we are dealing with and bring it to the Lord Jesus.

CHAPTER NINE

WHOSE HAND IS ON DAVID?

 n every human heart lies the possibility to desire evil to come to someone else. Have you ever been angry with someone, and you wanted harm to come to that person? It is possible for our old nature, like an evil beast, to strike back with vengeance.

A human drama unfolds for us in the closing part of the eighteenth chapter of I Samuel, revealing to us much more than what is happening in this one story. Often as we behold the behavior of others, the Lord speaks to us about our sinful ways. In this passage, two men display their behavior. One, the Bible declares, behaves himself wisely. The other man behaves himself in an evil fashion. As we take a discerning look at both of their lives, we see not only what is happening on this occasion, but we also discover where each kind of behavior leads. One man obviously had God's blessing on his life while the other man was rejected by the Lord.

Whose Hand Is on David?

The story of David and Saul continues in I Samuel 18:15-23,

> *Wherefore when Saul saw that he behaved himself very wisely, he was afraid of him. But all Israel and Judah loved David, because he went out and came in before them. And Saul said to David, Behold my elder daughter Merab, her will I give thee to wife: only be thou valiant for me, and fight the LORD's battles. For Saul said, Let not mine hand be upon him, but let the hand of the Philistines be upon him. And David said unto Saul, Who am I? and what is my life, or my father's family in Israel, that I should be son in law to the king? But it came to pass at the time when Merab Saul's daughter should have been given to David, that she was given unto Adriel the Meholathite to wife. And Michal Saul's daughter loved David: and they told Saul, and the thing pleased him. And Saul said, I will give him her, that she may be a snare to him, and that the hand of the Philistines may be against him. Wherefore Saul said to David, Thou shalt this day be my son in law in the one of the twain. And Saul commanded his servants, saying, Commune with David secretly, and say, Behold, the king hath delight in thee, and all his servants love thee: now therefore be the king's son in law. And Saul's servants spake those words in the ears of David. And David said, Seemeth it to you a light thing to be a king's son in law, seeing that I am a poor man, and lightly esteemed?*

Notice verses twenty-eight through thirty,

> *And Saul saw and knew that the LORD was with David, and that Michal Saul's daughter loved him. And Saul was yet the more afraid of David, and Saul became David's enemy continually. Then the princes*

of the Philistines went forth: and it came to pass, after they went forth, that David behaved himself more wisely than all the servants of Saul; so that his name was much set by.

Our God desires to teach us. Are we willing to learn what He desires to teach us? As we take a close look at the lives of these two men, we will learn some very valuable lessons.

Looking at the life of Saul, we notice things we do not want in our lives. Looking at the life of David, we notice things we do want. In the Christian life, we talk so much about men and God, and rightly so. However, that is not the way most people view life. People do not look at life between men and God; people view life between men and other men.

> *Often as we behold the behavior of others, the Lord speaks to us about our sinful ways.*

We are saying loudly and clearly what we believe about God by the way we treat people. We tell people what we believe about God by the way we act when other people affect our lives.

These two men testify about God by the way they respond to each other. As you read this passage carefully, you are going to notice again and again that Saul talks about his hand and the hand of the Philistines. He said, "I don't want my hand on David, or at least I don't want anyone to think my hand is on him. I want the hand of the Philistines to be on him."

We soon understand whose hand is on David. It is not the hand of Saul, nor the hand of the Philistines, but the hand of God and the hand of God's blessing. On occasion, we see people or perhaps meet people, and we recognize the hand of God upon them. If there is something we could do to have God's hand on our lives, would it not be a wonderful thing to do? More than anything else may the desire of our hearts be to have God's hand on our lives. This takes care of all else.

You do not have to be a preacher to have God's hand on your life. As a matter of fact, many do not! For example, I know some widows who have God's hand on their lives. They are cared for miraculously. You cannot explain how everything happens for them, except to say that God's hand is on their lives.

I know some young couples who have God's hand on their lives. You cannot explain what is going on in their lives without saying, "God's hand is on them." I also know some young people who have God's hand on their lives because you cannot explain what is happening in their lives, and what is coming to them, except to say that the hand of God is upon them. I know businessmen and women who have God's hand on their lives. It is obvious that God is blessing them and leading them.

> *We are saying loudly and clearly what we believe about God by the way we treat people. We tell people what we believe about God by the way we act when other people affect our lives.*

How strange to live in a world that denies the very existence of God, among people who do not recognize God, and yet those of us who have been born again by the Spirit of God can see through our spiritual eyes when God's hand is on someone! Whose hand was on David? It was God's hand.

It is terrible to desire evil to happen to someone. Not long ago, word came to me about a particular man who had sworn that whatever it took, he would spare no expense to destroy another man's life. I thought to myself, "What has happened in a man's heart, who says he is a Christian, to cause him to make that kind of statement?"

He said that he would spare no expense; he would do anything and everything possible in his power to destroy another man's life. In a short period of time, the man who vowed to destroy another man was dead himself. This is exactly what we find in the story of Saul and David.

May I make it simple for you? Either we have God's hand on our lives or we do not. There is no middle ground. It is just this simple. Is God's hand on your life? God's hand was on the life of David.

THE FOOLISHNESS OF KING SAUL

If you will notice in I Samuel 18:8, Saul had heard the song, "David has killed his ten thousands, and Saul has only killed his thousands." Saul was not willing to dance to that tune. Every time he heard the women singing, "Saul has killed his thousands, but David has killed his ten thousands," he became angry. It made him so angry he declared, "I will do anything I can do to put an end to David's life." He tried to kill David himself; but God delivered David from Saul.

Saul had promised to give David one of his daughters. Then the daughter he started to give him, he gave to another man. Saul said, "I will give him another one of my daughters." Saul arranged the wedding in such a fashion that the whole thing would be a snare to David's life.

If you read the entire story of this episode in David's life, you will discover that it did not turn out to be a snare to him. The daughter he finally married helped deliver David. God took care of David.

Saul said, "I am not going to require a dowry, David. I am going to tell you what I want. If you want to marry my daughter, I want some of my enemies killed. I want you to kill one hundred of these uncircumcised Philistines for me." He was hoping of course that one of them would kill David. He then said, "I want you to bring evidence to me that you have killed one hundred of them." All the while, he was hoping that they would kill David.

To make a long story short, David went out with other men and killed not one hundred of the enemy but two hundred. He brought to Saul evidence of the two hundred slain. When he came back unharmed before King Saul, the Bible says in verse twenty-eight, *"And Saul saw and knew that the LORD was with David, and that Michal Saul's daughter loved him."*

> *We soon understand whose hand is on David. It is not the hand of Saul, nor the hand of the Philistines, but the hand of God and the hand of God's blessing.*

Saul thought, "I have tried again and failed." Saul had planned for the Philistines to kill David. After all of Saul's fruitless attempts to take the life of David, the Bible says in I Samuel 26:21, *"Then said Saul, I have sinned: return, my son David: for I will no more do thee harm, because my soul was precious in thine eyes this day: behold, I have played the fool, and have erred exceedingly."*

If you will turn to the closing chapter of this book, you will find that it was not David who was slain in battle with the Philistines; it was Saul.

Here is a lesson we need to learn. The most foolish thing on earth for anyone to ever try to do is to play God and attempt to execute judgment on some other human being's life. There is nothing more foolish for a Christian to do than to try to get even with someone. God said in Deuteronomy 32:35, *"To me belongeth vengeance."*

There is nothing more evil for a child of God to do than to try to hurt someone else. That intention is like a boomerang. You may throw it at someone else, but I guarantee you the Bible is true and it will come back to strike you, or me, if we throw it.

When I was reading through this, I nearly wept as Saul talked to David in I Samuel 18:17. He said to David, "I want you to fight the Lord's battles." This man cared nothing about the Lord and the Lord's battles, but he employed this religious talk.

When you or I get something in our heart toward another human being that should not be there, we start living the life of a hypocrite. Jealousy destroys the vessel in which it is contained.

You may get angry with your wife and try to get even with her. You may get angry with your husband and try to get even with him. The truth of the matter is, you are going to hurt yourself every time. You may get angry with someone at work and attempt to get even with that person. You may get angry with someone in church and try to hurt him or do harm to him. That is foolish because it always comes back on you.

Whose hand was on David? God is going to make sure that His children, who have His hand on them, are protected. King Saul was foolish. He said, "I have played the fool."

THE FAITH OF DAVID

Talking about God is not the only way a man can express his faith. You can tell if someone is a genuine Christian who loves God by the way he talks about other people.

A man does not have to stand and say, "I have faith in God." It is a great thing to say, and he should say it; but he does not have to stand up and say that he has faith in God to demonstrate his faith in God. He can demonstrate that he has faith in God by the way he lives. The

Bible says in John 13:35, *"By this shall all men know that ye are my disciples, if ye have love one to another."*

Do you know the Lord as your personal Savior? Have you asked Him to forgive your sin and by faith received Him as your Savior? Do you know if you died today that you would go to heaven? Then the life you live should demonstrate faith in God.

Here is a lesson we need to learn. The most foolish thing on earth for anyone to ever try to do is to play God and attempt to execute judgment on some other human being's life. There is nothing more foolish for a Christian to do than to try to get even with someone.

David never sought the kingdom of Israel. David never lifted one finger to become king. He sought the Lord, and the Lord gave him the throne of Israel.

This is a good lesson for young men and women who are not married. You do not have to go out and find a mate. You do not have to seek a mate like someone on a scavenger hunt. That is the way the unsaved behave, but that is not the way Christians should behave themselves. You do not have to find the best-looking person in town. It is not that way with a child of God. The child of God demonstrates his faith in God by the way he responds to other people. If you put God first and seek God, He will bring into your life the person He wants you to have. This is the way God works.

David did not seek to be the son-in-law of the king. He sought the Lord, and God made him the son-in-law of the king. A person's faith in God or lack of it is demonstrated every day he lives. Do you know that the way you do your day's work on the job demonstrates your faith in God or lack of faith in God? Do you know that how you and I respond to authority demonstrates our faith in God or lack of faith in God? How we treat our families demonstrates our faith in God or lack of it. How we respond to our children demonstrates our faith in God or lack of it.

In Psalm 55, David wrote about his enemies. He had King Saul in mind here. In Psalm 55:16-21 he says,

> *As for me, I will call upon God; and the LORD shall save me. Evening, and morning, and at noon, will I pray, and cry aloud: and he shall hear my voice. He hath delivered my soul in peace from the battle that was against me: for there were many with me. God shall hear, and afflict them, even he that abideth of old. Selah. Because they have no changes, therefore they fear not God. He hath put forth his hands against such as be at peace with him: he hath broken his covenant. The words of his mouth were smoother than butter, but war was in his heart: his words were softer than oil, yet were they drawn swords.*

Saul secretly told his servants, "Go tell him that I love him. Go tell him that we all love him. I can't tell him that because he will not believe me. I tried to pin him to the wall with a spear and kill him, but go tell him secretly that we are all talking about him up here in the king's palace." David said that his words were smooth like butter and oil, but in reality they were swords, drawn swords.

> *Jealousy destroys the vessel in which it is contained.*

In verses twenty-two and twenty-three he says, *"Cast thy burden upon the LORD, and he shall sustain thee: he shall never suffer the righteous to be moved. But thou, O God, shalt bring them down into the pit of destruction: bloody and deceitful men shall not live out half their days; but I will trust in thee."*

David had faith in God. We see the foolishness of Saul and the faith of David. How are you going to live? There are people even in good, Bible-believing, Bible-preaching churches who are living like Saul. They are trying to get even with people, or wishing harm would come to them. May God help all of us to live with faith in God as David did.

THE FAITHFULNESS OF GOD

God did not let David down. The Lord was faithful to him. If you will look again in I Samuel 18:28-29, the Bible says, *"And Saul saw and knew that the LORD was with David, and that Michal Saul's daughter loved him. And Saul was yet the more afraid of David."*

I have this expression marked in my Bible because Saul should have been afraid of God, not David. When people fear God, they do not fear people. What harm can people do to me if I am trusting in the Lord? Nothing can come to me except what God allows.

Do you realize that we can live the Christian life with God guiding us, caring for us, protecting us, and providing for us?

The Bible says that when old Abraham was down in Egypt, the king of Egypt said, "We see that the Lord is with you." The Bible says that when Joseph was in the house of Potiphar, Potiphar said, "Joseph, we see that God is with you." In the days of David, the hand of the Lord was upon him.

The Bible says in verse thirty, *"Then the princes of the Philistines went forth: and it came to pass, after they went forth, that David behaved himself more wisely than all the servants of Saul; so that his name was much set by."*

David became precious to those servants because God's hand was on his life. If there is something in your life or my life that crowds out God's blessing, we should run to God and cry, "Help me!" For yourself, for your own soul, for your children, for peace of heart, and for the opportunity to pray, if there is anything in your life that is not right with God, cry out to God, "Lord, cleanse me. May Your hand of blessing be on me. Cleanse me so I can be what You want me to be, and have from Your good hand to my life what You want me to have."

Will you live like Saul or like David? Will you live a life of faith or the life of a fool? Have faith in God!

CHAPTER TEN

WHEN IT IS TIME TO TALK TO THE PREACHER

he secret was out. King Saul wanted David dead. He had started talking about it openly. In I Samuel 19:1 the Bible says, *"And Saul spake to Jonathan his son, and to all his servants, that they should kill David."*

Much was going on in the life of David, and there are many things God tells us in these brief chapters. When we come to I Samuel 19:18 the Bible says, *"So David fled, and escaped, and came to Samuel to Ramah, and told him all that Saul had done to him. And he and Samuel went and dwelt in Naioth."* There came a time in the life of David when he knew he must talk to the preacher. He sought out Samuel. God gives us those who watch for our souls (Hebrews 13:17).

Saul sat on the throne of Israel as a rejected king. Samuel had always been troubled about this man Saul, but especially now. God assured the prophet that He was going to do something about it.

He led Samuel to Bethlehem to the house of Jesse, and Samuel anointed David to be king over Israel someday. God worked it out so that David was in the care of the king of Israel. King Saul became jealous of David and desired to take his life. As all these disrupting things were happening in the life of David, the thought came to his mind, "If I could find the prophet, if I could just talk to the preacher, I believe I could get help." One day Samuel looked up, and David stood at his door.

> *We live our lives one day at a time. Every day we live is a part of our lifetime, and what happens in that day is a piece of the whole which God puts together for all of life; but God has more for us than the events of one day.*

I have looked up many times during my years in the ministry and have seen all kinds of people at my door. I have seen people with tears in their eyes saying, "My baby died today," or "We just got back from the doctor and found out that my wife has cancer and is terminally ill." I have heard people say, "My husband has an inoperable brain tumor, and I do not know what we are going to do," or "Pastor, our boy left home last night, and we can't find him," or "My daughter ran away and I have no idea where she is," or "My husband left me and these children, and we don't know where to turn." I have had all kinds of messages brought to me from hurting people.

On the other side of that coin, there are many grand things that people have had to talk about. "My boy came home." "My husband just got saved." "The doctor gave us a wonderful report." "My child is going to live." "My husband came home and asked me to forgive him, and I did. We wept and cried and praised God together, and things are going to be all right." If you are a minister of the gospel, if you are trying to serve the Lord, there are going to be many people appear at your door with many things on their hearts.

We live in a world of sorrow and heartache. There is no way to escape it. People who are hurting need to hear God's voice and try to find out what God is doing. What is the Lord saying to them?

When David appeared at Samuel's door, he was looking for counsel. He needed advice. The Bible says in Proverbs 1:5, *"A wise man will hear, and will increase learning; and a man of understanding shall attain unto wise counsels."*

David knew that he needed counsel, and the Bible says, *"A man of understanding shall attain unto wise counsels."* He said, "I need to talk to someone. I am having a hard time. I need counsel." So he went to his preacher, Samuel.

Samuel was an old man who had served God for years. His life had been totally given to the Lord. As a matter of fact, his mother gave him to God before his birth. His mother took him to Eli in the tabernacle to be brought up from childhood for the Lord and for the Lord's glory.

I hurt when I think that so many people across the world have lost confidence in preachers. Some men are deserving of that loss of confidence, but there are many men who are serving the Lord from their hearts. They are trying to walk before God day by day. We should pray for preachers. We should hold them up in our prayers and in our conversation. We should thank God for people who believe the Bible and are trying to live the truth and preach the truth.

David also needed comfort. Perhaps he needed an arm around his shoulder. God knows sometimes that we need comforting. David ran to Ramah to where Samuel was dwelling because he knew that being with Samuel would bring comfort.

He also needed companionship. He needed someone he could talk to about the things of the Lord. He needed to talk to someone who understood what was going on in his heart. He needed to be able to say, "I love God, and I want to serve God." He needed someone with a listening ear who would understand.

Sometimes we talk to people about the things of the Lord, and we know when we are talking that they have no idea what we are talking about. David needed companionship. He needed to see someone who understood that he did love God, was trying to serve God, and was trying to live for God. He wanted to talk to someone who loved God, feared God, and was trying to live for God. That is why he sought out the preacher.

> *That visit to Samuel was a help to David. He found counsel, comfort, and companionship. I want us to look at what brought him there, because it is so difficult for us to see God in the bad things.*

That visit to Samuel was a help to David. He found counsel, comfort, and companionship. I want us to look at what brought him there, because it is so difficult for us to see God in the bad things. When we see the end of the thing, and if we are drawn close to God because of it, we praise God for it. However, it is so hard when things are going the wrong way to see God in it. This is what this part of the story is all about.

We live our lives one day at a time. Every day we live is a part of our lifetime, and what happens in that day is a piece of the whole which God puts together for all of life; but God has more for us than the events of one day. God has more for us than the news from a doctor, or the news from a family member, or the news from someone with whom we work. There is more to life than one announcement. This is not the end of it.

If you are a Christian, you are headed to heaven. Someday we are going to lay down this robe of flesh and soar beyond the stars. We are going to breathe the air of glory, step on a street of gold, and see the face of our Lord Jesus. Then we will be so ashamed of anything that distracted us down here.

THE BURDEN ON DAVID

Here we find a shepherd boy minding his own business, obeying his father. He went to the valley of Elah and was used of God to kill the Philistine giant and deliver the nation of Israel. One would think that all who knew him would be singing his praises, but David had a difficult time.

The Bible begins to tell us about the struggles he was having at the hand of Saul. When Saul had jealousy spring up in his heart, he could have given the matter to God, put it under foot, and stomped it out. When he had this spark of jealousy spring up in his heart, he could have extinguished it in a season of prayer. He could have prayed, "God, help me. I must not feel this way."

Many times we look on things in life and think, "Why did God let it go to that extreme?" Notice the burden on David's life. In I Samuel 18:11 we read, *"Saul cast the javelin; for he said, I will smite David even to the wall with it."* Saul tried to kill him with a javelin. Saul was a soldier, a man of tremendous ability. If he wanted to kill, he could kill. The only reason he did not kill David was that God delivered David.

The Bible says that Saul could not kill David with a javelin, so in verse thirteen we read, *"Therefore Saul removed him from him, and made him his captain over a thousand."* Saul wanted David to go out and fight because he thought someone would kill him in battle. Then he encouraged David to go fight the Philistines. This was not because he wanted the Philistines defeated; rather he wanted

David dead. Men can go to such terrible depths. Then Saul said, "I am going to give you the daughter I promised you when you killed Goliath." He gave him the daughter, Merab, and then took her away. Can you imagine that?

Then Saul had another idea. He had one daughter named Michal whom he thought would be a snare to David. In verse twenty-one Saul said, *"And I will give him her, that she may be a snare to him."* In other words, he was saying, "I have had enough problems out of that girl. I am going to give her to David and let her destroy his life." He gave Michal to David on the condition that David go out and kill one hundred Philistines and bring evidence of it back to him. In the twenty-fifth verse the Bible says, *"Thus shall ye say to David, The king desireth not any dowry, but an hundred foreskins of the Philistines."*

Saul was hoping all the time that one of those Philistines would kill David. Remember that instead of David killing one hundred, he killed two hundred of them and brought back evidence to Saul.

Then David got the news through Jonathan that Saul had told the people in his court that he wanted David dead. Jonathan said, "David, you had better get out of here. I am going to talk to dad tomorrow, and I want you hiding near enough to hear what we are saying. If I can convince him not to kill you, I will call you out from where you are hiding."

Jonathan talked Saul into going out for a conversation. David was hiding near enough to hear them. Jonathan said to his dad, "David delivered us from the hand of the Philistines. He killed the giant. He delivered Israel. You must not kill him." Saul said, "I have made a mistake. I will not kill him." Jonathan said, "David, come on out. Everything is going to be all right from now on."

They took David back into the king's court, and David started playing the harp again. While David had the harp in his hand, Saul put a javelin back in his hand and tried to kill him again, but missed.

When David went home to Michal, Saul told his servants, "I want you to get David while he is sleeping in the bed and kill him." Verse eleven of I Samuel 19 says, *"Saul also sent messengers unto David's house, to watch him, and to slay him in the morning."*

Most Bible students believe that the fifty-ninth Psalm was written as a result of this attempt on David's life at the hands of Saul and his soldiers. Michal disguised something in the bed, and let David down by a rope out the window. David fled, and when the soldiers finally came in, she lied and said, "David was going to kill me. Tell the king that David said he was going to kill me. That is why I had to let him go."

This is some of the trouble that David was living in. I am sure there were many times when he thought, "I would be much better off if I had stayed in Bethlehem and had never seen that giant."

There was a great burden on David's life, but there is something of which we must make note–God allowed it. I am not trying to tell you that I understand this. I am not trying to tell you that God is a bully pushing people around and doing bad things to them. However, I am saying that there is a God in heaven who allowed this.

You may say, "I am having a hard time." The Bible says in Job 14:1, *"Man that is born of a woman is of few days and full of trouble."* Everyone who has ever lived has had a hard time. Life is not all a burden, but there are burdens in life that we are called to bear.

THE BREAKING OF DAVID

I have tried to get acquainted with David. He is mentioned over one thousand times in the Bible. David became an independent sort of man. You do not kill a giant and deliver a nation without having some things to deal with concerning your self-sufficiency and independence. How can a man who could do everything himself ever depend on God? True *independence* in the life of a believer means true *dependence* upon God.

David was a man after God's own heart. This kind of dedication is a daily matter. I cannot live on past victories. I cannot live my Christian life on what I accomplished years ago. I cannot live a victorious Christian life on what God did yesterday. It is a daily matter.

> *True independence in the life of a believer means true dependence upon God.*

Who did David need? He killed a lion and a bear with his own hands. He killed a giant with a sling and a stone. Who did he need? As we follow David's life, remember that David was on his way to the throne.

When David was let down out of the window and escaped to Ramah, with every step he took to Samuel's house, he thought, "Lord, what are You doing in my life?" But with every step he took toward that prophet's house, he was moving closer and closer to a place of dependence upon God.

My family and I lived just a few miles from New York City for eight years. Occasionally, when we were in New York City, we would see men building a great skyscraper. You would not believe what it looks like when they start building on that island. You would think that a bomb had been dropped, and a crater the size of a massive building had been created in the earth. They were going as deep as they needed to go because they were going higher than you ever imagined. When I go back and see those massive buildings that stand so tall, I recall those great holes that were made for foundations. Then I realize it took that kind of foundation to make a building that great.

If you and I ever expect God to do something out of the ordinary with our lives, then we need to expect God to prepare a solid foundation in us. We think that we should have a great marriage without ever having to deal with any problems. We think that we should have a great church without ever having to deal with any problems. We think that we should have a great life without ever having to deal with any problems. It does not work this way. It never has and it never will, not in our personal lives, our children, or any other area of life.

God brings us to a place of dependence upon Him. There is a breaking of life before the blessings.

THE BLESSINGS ON DAVID

I do not want to hurt. I do not want to suffer or be in pain. I do not even want to be pricked by a thorn. I do not want it, but I know how God works. God deals with us not to hurt us but to help us.

No one is in a better position than the one who is nearest God. God allows what is necessary to bring us near to Him.

The blessing on David's life was only a taste of what was to come. Look what happened when he went to see Samuel. The Bible says in I Samuel 19:19-20,

> *And it was told Saul, saying, Behold, David is at Naioth in Ramah. And Saul sent messengers to take David: and when they saw the company of the prophets prophesying, and Samuel standing as appointed over them, the Spirit of God was upon the messengers of Saul, and they also prophesied.*

Can you imagine this scene? God was blessing in a mighty way with David, and Samuel, and the school of the prophets. By the way, Samuel started the school of the prophets. Samuel was a man who served God, knew God, and loved God. He surrounded himself with young people who wanted to serve God and do the will of God. This became the school of the prophets. When David went to see Samuel, he also got near the school of the prophets. If you asked David, from his perspective one thing was going on. If you asked Samuel, from his perspective he saw something entirely different going on. If you asked from the perspective of the school of the prophets, they saw another thing happening.

The young men in the school of the prophets would say, "We are seeing how God works, how God gets things done, and how God deals with the king. We are seeing how the preacher advises a king. We are looking at it from that perspective." If you looked at it from Samuel's

No one is in a better position than the one who is nearest God. God allows what is necessary to bring us near to Him.

perspective, Samuel would say, "I am seeing that God even deals with a king. God is preparing David for the throne, and I am glad that these preacher boys can see what God is doing." If you looked at it from David's perspective, David would say, "I am seeing that God is able, in these situations where I am so perplexed and distressed, to see me through."

Then suddenly, Saul's soldiers arrived. God's presence was so mightily upon the place that they were blessed. Saul became so disturbed that he sent another group out, and they were blessed. Finally, Saul himself said, "I am going to take this thing into my own hands. I am going to go find out what is going on." Saul went there and God was working so mightily that Saul was blessed and started to prophesy.

God wants to bless all of us. He wants to do something so mighty that everyone can get in on His blessings.

It was time to see the preacher. David left and went to Ramah, and he and Samuel left Ramah and went to Naioth, and they worshipped God. If you could have eavesdropped on that meeting with Samuel and David, you would have found out something very unique. In that meeting with Samuel and David, both of them knew all about Saul. From what we find in the Bible, we understand that they were talking more about God than they were talking about Saul. What they did, no doubt, was start talking about the Lord and praising God, and God started blessing.

May the Lord of heaven and earth help us to learn this lesson. We are not going to live in this world without trouble. One is not going to pastor the church I pastor without burdens to bear. Our members are not going to be a part of the church without part of that burden to bear. However, there is a God in heaven who wants to bless us. In the midst of all our difficulties, He wants to bless us if we will only look at Him and not at the trouble. Our trouble is only a method He uses to bring us to Himself.

If you are in the middle of trouble, have you looked to the Lord yet? I believe that when David turned toward God's man, he was actually saying in his heart, "I am turning toward God." No wonder Jesus Christ stands with open arms and says, *"Come unto me, all ye that labour and are heavy laden, and I will give you rest."* Run into His arms. You need that rest.

CHAPTER ELEVEN

DEATH IS BUT A STEP AWAY

here are so many things about the life of David that God uses to speak to each of us. Our eyes are to move from David to David's God. David had become a very discouraged man. He had come to one of those moments in life in which he felt as if the wicked were going to win. Perhaps you have had some of those moments in your life. David needed to reconsider the fact that his life was truly in the hands of God.

The Bible says in I Samuel 20:1-3,

> *And David fled from Naioth in Ramah, and came and said before Jonathan, What have I done? what is mine iniquity? and what is my sin before thy father, that he seeketh my life? And he said unto him, God forbid; thou shalt not die: behold, my father will do nothing either great or small, but that he will shew it me: and why should my father hide this thing from*

me? it is not so. And David sware moreover, and said, Thy father certainly knoweth that I have found grace in thine eyes; and he saith, Let not Jonathan know this, lest he be grieved: but truly as the LORD liveth, and as thy soul liveth, there is but a step between me and death.

David felt that his own life was in such jeopardy that, with his next breath, his life could be taken. He said, *"There is but a step between me and death."* In this conversation with Jonathan, the son of Saul, David said, "Tell me; I want to know what is going on. What is racing through your father's mind? What have I done that is so terrible that he wants to kill me?"

> *Discouraged people always overstate their problems.*

Jonathan, in an effort to comfort David, said, "David, I don't believe you are going to be killed. You are not going to die. If my father had intent to kill you, he would have told me." Soon Jonathan found that his father did intend to kill David.

Remember that the prophet Samuel told David that God had chosen him to be the next king of Israel. How could he possibly die before he came to the throne? Yet David said, *"There is but a step between me and death."* This was a lapse in David's faith. Discouraged people always overstate their problems.

Of course if the Lord does not come soon, we are all going to die. It is not a matter of if we are going to die, it is a matter of when we are going to die. It is going to happen. The Bible says, *"It is appointed unto men once to die."* Death is but a step away.

David was discouraged and he overstated his problem. We need to be careful about what we say when we are discouraged, because when we are discouraged we might say things that make matters much worse than they really are.

David took his eyes off the Lord and convinced Jonathan to tell a lie. Instead of relying on the Lord, David started scheming and planning. He said, "I want you to lie to your father. Go to the table and eat with your father. My place will be empty. Tell your father that I am away in Bethlehem with my father, Jesse, and my brothers and sisters. We have to find out what is in your father's heart." He schemed, and he got Jonathan to join in his scheme and to lie. The Christian must determine to live by faith and not by sight.

Peace With God

David stated that death was just a step away. If death truly is just a step away, there are some things that we should take care of now before we step into that moment of death. We need to make peace with God before we die.

God wants us to make peace with Him. He wants us to recognize that we are sinners, ask Him to forgive our sin, and by faith receive Jesus Christ as our Savior. He wants us to make sure, before we die, that we have trusted Him as our Savior and that heaven is our home. If we have not done that, in a moment, we could meet death, and eternity would be settled. We would be without Christ forever.

The Bible says in Colossians 1:20, *"And, having made peace through the blood of his cross, by him to reconcile all things unto himself; by him, I say, whether they be things in earth, or things in heaven."*

How do people make peace with God? The Bible says, *"...having made peace through the blood of his cross..."* By asking God to forgive our sin, trusting in the finished work of Jesus Christ, acknowledging that we cannot save ourselves, and asking the Lord Jesus Christ to save us, we can have peace with God.

Peace With Others

We should make peace with other people. Before we die, we need to make peace with other people. The Bible says in Romans 12:17-18, *"Recompense to no man evil for evil. Provide things honest in the sight of all men. If it be possible, as much as lieth in you, live peaceably with all men."*

It is tragic to have had the opportunity to make peace with people and having not done so, seal the death of that opportunity forever. Think of those with whom you have a problem. If you knew that you were going to die soon, would you not do all within your power to make peace with them?

Peace Within

We also need peace in our own hearts. The Bible says in Colossians 3:15, *"And let the peace of God rule in your hearts, to the which also ye are called in one body; and be ye thankful."* We should be doing with our lives what God wants us to do. If we are out of fellowship with the Lord, not where God wants us to be, not doing what He wants us to do, then by all means, let us take care of it before we meet the Lord. We can have peace in our hearts.

There are many things I would like to do with my life before I die. There are many things I would like to try to accomplish with my life before I die. The truth is that I have a peace in my heart knowing that I am doing what God wants me to do day by day.

It is true that death is but one step away. Our next breath could be our last. Let us make peace with God, peace with others, and have peace within our own hearts. We can have peace with God through salvation, peace with others through forgiveness, and peace in our own hearts through obedience to the will of God.

David said that death was but one step away. What lies between us and death? Who can say we will take another breath? My friend, Bill

124

Rivenburg, who worked with me in the ministry at Madison Avenue Baptist Church, was working in a room sweeping the floor when his heart failed; he was dead before his body hit the floor. Before he fell to the floor, he was in the presence of God.

If death is certain, and it is, then what is between us and death? What lies there in that space?

THE PROVISION OF GOD

The word *providence* frightens some people. There are a number of ways to use this word. You will not find the word in your Bible, but by the providence of God, we mean the provision of God. In this sense, we speak of the way God takes care of us.

In I Samuel 20:1 the Bible says, *"And David fled from Naioth in Ramah, and came and said before Jonathan, What have I done? what is mine iniquity? and what is my sin before thy father, that he seeketh my life? And he said unto him, God forbid; thou shalt not die."* What caused Jonathan to say that David would not die? Who could say such a thing? The javelin had been thrown at David, and would soon be thrown at Jonathan in Saul's anger. What made Jonathan say that David would not die? It was because Jonathan had already realized, in the providential care of God, that David was going to be the king of Israel. He felt that God had already made that decision about the life of David. He knew that David was under the care and keeping of Almighty God, and nothing could come to David unless God allowed it to come.

Nothing will come to me that might be considered harmful, unless God allows it to come. Between me and death lies the providential care of almighty God.

Looking at the life of David, why do you think that David went into a cave, and Saul came into that same cave? David could have killed

Saul, but Saul could have killed David. Was it just a coincidence that they went into the same cave? No, it was the providential care of God. God is always at work, on our behalf, through the Lord Jesus Christ. Our God is in control.

When we think about the birth of our Savior, we remember Caesar Augustus, who made the decree that all the world should be taxed. In this story, we find a Roman emperor sitting on the throne, thinking of himself as the mightiest man in the world. At a certain moment in human history he made a decree that all the world should be taxed. Mary and Joseph, simple peasant people, made a journey to Bethlehem. Hundreds of years earlier, God had said that Jesus Christ would be born in Bethlehem. Did they just happen to travel to Bethlehem, the place of their ancestry, because Caesar Augustus made his decree? The truth of the matter is that the work of God is the focal point of human history, and Caesar Augustus, Roman ruler of the world, was nothing more than a piece of lint on a page of history compared to what God was doing. God is almighty, and between me and death lies the providential care and keeping of our God. I will not spend the rest of my life worrying about how I am going to die or when I am going to die, if I keep my eyes on Jesus Christ and His care for me.

> *Between me and death lies the providential care of almighty God.*

THE PROTECTING HAND OF GOD

As we look for God in His providential care and provision, we can see just beyond that how He protects us. We do not know how many times we have been spared from death, but I believe we have been spared. We do not know how many times we have been spared from some disease that could have been life threatening, but we have been

126

spared. I cannot fully understand the mind and heart of God, but I do know that I live under His protecting hand.

In Isaiah 54:17 the Bible says,

> *No weapon that is formed against thee shall prosper; and every tongue that shall rise against thee in judgment thou shalt condemn. This is the heritage of the servants of the LORD, and their righteousness is of me, saith the LORD.*

God says, *"No weapon that is formed against thee shall prosper."* Why? God is protecting us. Another place where we find mention of God's protection is in Psalm 91. The Bible says in verses one through seven,

> *He that dwelleth in the secret place of the Most High shall abide under the shadow of the Almighty. I will say of the LORD, He is my refuge and my fortress: my God; in him will I trust. Surely he shall deliver thee from the snare of the fowler, and from the noisome pestilence. He shall cover thee with his feathers, and under his wings shalt thou trust: his truth shall be thy shield and buckler. Thou shalt not be afraid for the terror by night; nor for the arrow that flieth by day; nor for the pestilence that walketh in darkness; nor for the destruction that wasteth at noonday. A thousand shall fall at thy side, and ten thousand at thy right hand; but it shall not come nigh thee.*

Between me and death, between this moment and the step that I shall take that shall be my last step, lies the protecting hand of God upon my life. I am in a place of safety in the will of God. This is why we say to people who are going to the mission field or other places around the world to serve the Lord, "Do not fear if you know you are doing God's will. If He calls you to work among some primitive tribe of people, do not fret. If you are in God's will, that is the place of safety."

David said, *"There is but a step between me and death,"* but thank God in that step we find the providing and the protecting hand of God. In Psalm eight, the Bible says in verses one through four,

> *The work of God is the focal point of human history, and Caesar Augustus, Roman ruler of the world, was nothing more than a piece of lint on a page of history compared to what God was doing.*

O LORD our Lord, how excellent is thy name in all the earth! who hast set thy glory above the heavens. Out of the mouth of babes and sucklings hast thou ordained strength because of thine enemies, that thou mightest still the enemy and the avenger. When I consider thy heavens, the work of thy fingers, the moon and the stars, which thou hast ordained; what is man, that thou art mindful of him? and the son of man, that thou visitest him?

"What is man...?" is given in the form of a question, but it is also a great statement of truth. The truth is that God is mindful of man. What does this mean? It means God is mindful of where I am at this moment, what I am doing today, what I am thinking today, what I face today, and what I will deal with the next moment.

God is mindful of me. I am His, and He loves me. I do not know of anything that encourages me more than knowing this. As you are having a hard time, remember, God is mindful of what you are going through. It is His desire to help you, and to be all you need.

David said, "There is but a step between me and death." If death is but a step away, rejoice that God's providing hand and His protecting hand is upon us.

THE PROMISES OF GOD

In that step between us and death, we have all of the promises of God. Do you need direction? He has a promise for it. Do you need comfort? He has a promise for it. Do you need provision? He has a promise for it. Do you need help for something or someone? He has a promise for it. You are not alone.

The Bible says in II Corinthians 1:20, *"For all the promises of God in him are yea, and in him Amen, unto the glory of God by us."* There was no reason for David to become so discouraged, because the truth is that God ordained him for the throne of Israel. He took care of him, delivering him from the lion, the bear, the giant, and the king. The promises of God are between all His children and death.

No wonder the Lord Jesus talked to His disciples like He did. He said to them in Matthew 6:25-34,

> *Therefore I say unto you, Take no thought for your life, or what ye shall eat, or what ye shall drink; nor yet for your body, what ye shall put on. Is not the life more than meat, and the body than raiment? Behold the fowls of the air: for they sow not, neither do they reap, nor gather into barns; yet your heavenly Father feedeth them. Are ye not much better than they? Which of you by taking thought can add one cubit unto his stature? And why take ye thought for raiment? Consider the lilies of the field, how they grow; they toil not, neither do they spin: and yet I say unto you, That even Solomon in all his glory was not arrayed like one of these. Wherefore, if God so*

clothe the grass of the field, which to day is, and to morrow is cast into the oven, shall he not much more clothe you, O ye of little faith? Therefore take no thought, saying, What shall we eat? or, What shall we drink? or, Wherewithal shall we be clothed? (For after all these things do the Gentiles seek:) for your heavenly Father knoweth that ye have need of all these things. But seek ye first the kingdom of God, and his righteousness; and all these things shall be added unto you. Take therefore no thought for the morrow: for the morrow shall take thought for the things of itself. Sufficient unto the day is the evil thereof.

It is very easy for me to talk about David saying to Jonathan, "Jonathan, your father is going to kill me." It is easy for me to say to David, "David, wake up! You are worrying about something you should not be worrying about." David said, "I am going to die, and I may die soon, because there is just a step between me and death.

I am in a place of safety in the will of God.

Saul is about to put an end to my life." It is easy for me to rebuke David, but God says to me, "Clarence Sexton, you wake up. You look up."

Between each of God's children and death lies all of our heavenly Father's care and keeping. He has kept us all so far, has He not? Someday when we get to heaven, we are going to find out that He may have delivered us from a hundred different things or more that could have taken our lives.

Between us and the end of this life are all the promises of God. If we need something, we must not worry and fret and complain. We must trust God.

If Christ does not return soon, we are going to die. We need to make peace with God and peace with others. However, we need to realize that between us and death we have the providing care of God, the protecting hand of God, and all the promises of God.

CHAPTER TWELVE

THE SCHOOL OF LONELINESS

here are moments in life when it seems that we are sinking so fast and so far that we are beyond recovery. When we open our Bibles to the twenty-first chapter of I Samuel, it appears that David was headed in that direction, going beyond the point of no return.

There are things in life that we choose for ourselves, but there are many other things that God chooses for us. When we come to grips with this truth, we are able to look beyond all secondary causes and see God's hand at work in our lives. Our God allows us to pass through periods of loneliness so that we might seek Him for all we need.

In the twenty-first chapter of I Samuel, we find David on the run. The Bible says in verses one through ten,

> *Then came David to Nob to Ahimelech the priest: and Ahimelech was afraid at the meeting of David, and said unto him, Why art thou alone, and no man with thee? And David said unto Ahimelech the priest,*

The king hath commanded me a business, and hath said unto me, Let no man know any thing of the business whereabout I send thee, and what I have commanded thee: and I have appointed my servants to such and such a place. Now therefore what is under thine hand? give me five loaves of bread in mine hand, or what there is present. And the priest answered David, and said, There is no common bread under mine hand, but there is hallowed bread; if the young men have kept themselves at least from women. And David answered the priest, and said unto him, Of a truth women have been kept from us about these three days, since I came out, and the vessels of the young men are holy, and the bread is in a manner common, yea, though it were sanctified this day in the vessel. So the priest gave him hallowed bread: for there was no bread there but the shewbread, that was taken from before the LORD, to put hot bread in the day when it was taken away. Now a certain man of the servants of Saul was there that day, detained before the LORD; and his name was Doeg, an Edomite, the chiefest of the herdmen that belonged to Saul. And David said unto Ahimelech, And is there not here under thine hand spear or sword? for I have neither brought my sword nor my weapons with me, because the king's business required haste. And the priest said, The sword of Goliath the Philistine, whom thou slewest in the valley of Elah, behold, it is here wrapped in a cloth behind the ephod: if thou wilt take that, take it: for there is no other save that here. And David said, There is none like that; give it me. And David arose, and fled that day for fear of Saul, and went to Achish the king of Gath.

Notice that Ahimelech asked David, *"Why art thou alone, and no man with thee?"*

I remind you again that some things in life we choose for ourselves. However, there is an ongoing part of life that God chooses for us. Believers in the Lord Jesus Christ can make a good decision in a moment, but it takes a lifetime to develop a dedicated Christian life, and there are certain things that God allows so that we can develop that dedicated Christian life.

David was on his way to the throne. He would be the king of Israel. He would eventually begin his forty-year reign, but everything on the way to the throne was preparation for what he was going to do, as God worked in his life. In this twenty-first chapter, we find David in the school of loneliness.

David was going to school again. This time, God put him in a school where he was all alone. There was a little village not very far from Jerusalem called Nob. The tabernacle was located there. There were eighty-six priests and their families who lived there. It was a relatively quiet place. David, fleeing from Saul, arrived at that village, and talked to Ahimelech the priest. While he was there he was stunned, because he was recognized by one of Saul's herdsmen.

> *All along life's journey, God prepares classrooms for His children in the school of loneliness.*

This herdsman was named Doeg. He was an Edomite, a man from Edom, a land across the Jordan River. He would later tell Saul what he had seen, and his report would cost the lives of eighty-five of those priests and all their families. This was all because David made an appearance that day at the village of Nob.

Some special things had been going on in David's life. God records that when he appeared at Nob, the priest asked him, "Why are you alone? Why are you here all by yourself?"

God prepares a school of loneliness for us. Sometimes the classroom is a hospital room, standing by the bed of someone you know and love. Sometimes the classroom is in your own home after everyone is gone and the children have left home. It could be after the desertion of a friend. Perhaps you are thinking about what you have done and cannot undo. At this point, God allows you to be in the school of loneliness.

> *As David walked off alone toward the wilderness, he entered into the school of loneliness.*

It may be when you report to your job, and you are told that your job no longer exists. You get in your car and start home, wondering what you are going to tell your wife and family. You have entered the school of loneliness. Sometimes it is in a ministry where you have made a decision, and people do not agree with your decision. Perhaps you have had a tough thing to deal with at home, and even your family members misunderstand you.

All along life's journey, God prepares classrooms for His children in the school of loneliness. Whether it is concern over a wayward child or dealing with some personal need in your life, God prepares a classroom. He says, "I want you to go to the school of loneliness for a while. There are some lessons that I want you to learn." He comes to meet us there.

In this Bible passage, we find that David had entered the school of loneliness. Back in the twentieth chapter of I Samuel, he had his companions, the greatest of whom was Jonathan, the son of the king. Notice carefully when you read again the twentieth chapter of I Samuel, David and Jonathan had met in the field as Jonathan shot an arrow near a certain stone. He was to give David a clue about whether he was to flee or to return to the king's palace. When Jonathan gave the word that David must leave and enter into exile, they were very distressed. After sending everyone else away, Jonathan embraced David and they wept. We are reminded in the last verse of the twentieth chapter of what they said,

> *And Jonathan said to David, Go in peace, forasmuch as we have sworn both of us in the name of the LORD, saying, The LORD be between me and thee, and between my seed and thy seed for ever. And he arose and departed: and Jonathan went into the city.*

David went one way, and Jonathan the other. Was this their last meeting until they met again in heaven? They would have one more encounter before Jonathan was killed in battle at the hand of the Philistines, at the same time his father Saul was killed.

Try to visualize the silhouette of a man stooped over, broken-hearted, and wondering what had gone wrong in life. As David walked off alone toward the wilderness, he entered into the school of loneliness.

The next time you feel as though you are all alone, think about what God wants to teach you in the school of loneliness. You may be in an environment filled with people, but you recognize God has enrolled you in the school of loneliness. What is He trying to teach you?

WE LEARN TO THINK

When we enter into the school of loneliness, the lessons begin. The first thing God wants us to do when we enter that classroom is to start thinking.

It is hard to think clearly as we are crowded by our daily routine. We rise from sleep every day and do many of the same things. We give greetings to the same people; we go through much of the same routine day after day. It is hard for people to stop and think about heaven, about hell, about eternity, about life, and about death when their lives are constantly crowded by increased activity.

> *God in heaven is able to get us all alone so that He is in the room with us, and it seems as if there is no one else in all the world but God. He causes us to think about what we need from Him.*

It is hard to slow people down to get them to think that they need a Savior. We are all sinners. If we die in our sin, we will not go to heaven. Jesus Christ came from heaven's glory to bleed and die upon the cross for us. He paid our sin debt. If we are willing to ask God to forgive our sin, and by faith receive the Lord Jesus as our Savior, He has promised to hear our prayer, forgive our sin, and save us.

I remember the day the doctor told my mother, "I am so sorry to have to tell you that your cancer has come back." When I talked to her on the phone she was crying. I spoke with her several times that day, and my brother, sisters, and other relatives talked to her. She told me, "That afternoon I said to every one, 'Leave me alone.'" She said to my brother, "I love you, but I want you to leave me alone." She said to Pop, "I love you, but I want to be left alone." She said to me, "I knew I had to be by myself. When I got by myself, I realized that God did love me, and that God would bring me through this like He brought me through before. His way is the best way. When I got alone, I was able to think. It took some time, but I thought through it."

Our Lord knows how to get our attention. I am not trying to point an accusing finger at anyone and say of anyone that this is something you need. Our God is able to get us all alone so that He is in the room with us, and it seems as if there is no one else in all the world but Him. He causes us to think about what we need from Him.

When we go to the school of loneliness, the first lesson we learn in the classroom is a lesson on how to think. Our thoughts are eventually, I hope, turned toward God.

WE LEARN THE SECRET OF STRENGTH

We are suffering today from a lack of strength as Christians. God works His greatest accomplishments in the lives of His people in hours of their great weakness and in hours of tremendous difficulty and darkness. The Bible says that His strength is made perfect in our weakness (II Corinthians 12:9).

David was not ready to rule Israel. He needed to be a much stronger man. What makes us strong? Does knowledge make us strong? Does physical ability make us strong? Do mental exercises make us strong? Remember, the Bible says that His strength is made perfect in our weakness. Men begin to know their weaknesses when they are all alone and they trust God for His strength.

Look at Abraham. In hours of loneliness, he found his strength in the Lord. Look at Joseph. As a seventeen-year-old boy, his brothers sold him to Midianite merchantmen. He went down to Egypt alone, separated from his father and his brethren. When he got to Egypt, he was cast into a dungeon all alone. God built strength of character into Joseph's life in the school of loneliness.

Look at Moses. God ordained that Moses lead the children of Israel from Egyptian bondage into the Promised Land. Moses was not ready to lead them as a forty-year-old man. When he fled into the desert after taking the life of an Egyptian, all alone with no one but God, the

Lord strengthened him to do the job God wanted him to do. Look at Daniel. He was also strengthened in the school of loneliness.

The thing that I do not want is the thing that I need most. The thing that I flinch from is the thing that God knows I need to make me strong. Trouble borne in the Spirit of Jesus Christ produces Christ-likeness. There is no painless way to follow the Son of God. This world is not our final home. The truth is that there are many things God wants to do in us and through us to strengthen us. He wants to build in us what we need to become the Christians He desires for us to be.

Come to the feet of Jesus Christ and say, "Lord, I am willing to submit, yield, and surrender to Your way in my time of difficulty. I know You want to teach me something to make me stronger. Help me, Lord Jesus, to be yielded to You." In the school of loneliness God desires to build strong Christians.

WE LEARN THAT WE ARE NEVER ALONE

David did a strange thing. Notice in the twenty-first chapter, that he was hungry. He was looking for food, for weapons, and for guidance. He found food, he found a weapon, but he did not get the guidance he needed.

He said to Ahimelech, "Do you have any spears or any swords here?" What a question to ask a priest. "Among those eighty-six priests there at Nob, do you have any weapons or armor?" He said in verse eight, *"And is there not here under thine hand spear or sword? for I have neither brought my sword nor my weapons with me, because the king's business required haste."*

David had been lying all the time. Saul had not sent him there. He was not on the king's business. The Bible continues in verse nine,

> *And the priest said, The sword of Goliath the Philistine, whom thou slewest in the valley of Elah, behold, it is here wrapped in a cloth behind the ephod: if thou wilt take that, take it: for there is no other save that here. And David said, There is none like that; give it me.*

David thought, "I want the sword of Goliath. That is what I need. If I have the weapon of the giant, I will be all right. If I have that great sword of Goliath, I can defend myself. I can defeat any foe if I just have that great sword of Goliath." That does not sound like the same David who in I Samuel 17:45 said, *"Thou comest to me with a sword, and with a spear, and with a shield: but I come to thee in the name of the LORD of hosts, the God of the armies of Israel, whom thou hast defied."*

There was a day when David trusted God saying, "I would rather have the Lord than have the sword." In chapter twenty-one he said, "I would rather have the sword than have the Lord." He had a lesson to learn.

When reading the Psalms, especially Psalms 34 and 52, which relate to this

Trouble borne in the Spirit of Jesus Christ produces Christ-likeness. There is no painless way to follow the Son of God.

time in David's life, we have revealed to us what David learned. God did not deliver him by the sword of Goliath. God delivered David the same way He delivered him in the valley of Elah when he fought Goliath. He was delivered by the strength of the Lord.

Often, when things go wrong, we start thinking, "How can I manipulate? How can I work on people? How can I convince a particular person? How can I use my influence and power? How can I use my position? How can I use all these things I possess to get people to do what I want them to do?"

Dr. Vance Havner said to me years ago, "We sing 'Christ is all I need,' but He is not really all we need until He is all we have; and when He is all we have, we find out He is all we need." The Lord wants us to realize when we are all alone, that we are never alone. He wants us to trust Him to help us. He said, *"I will never leave thee nor forsake thee"* (Hebrews 13:5).

David left Nob. He left Ahimelech the priest. He carried with him that great big sword of Goliath. He was alone, on his way to try to find a place to which he could flee from the wrath of King Saul. As I look on that scene, I think, "Oh, David, you are a better man than I will ever hope to be; but you are going to have to learn that a sword will not do. You must come to the place when you are on your face before God, trusting Him for what you need."

How many times my heavenly Father has looked upon me, and said, "Oh, my child, that is not the way. That is not the way to get it done. Trust Me. Lean on Me. Believe Me."

When the apostle Paul was writing his final words to Timothy, he said in II Timothy 4:16-18,

> *At my first answer no man stood with me, but all men forsook me: I pray God that it may not be laid to their charge. Notwithstanding the Lord stood with me, and strengthened me; that by me the preaching might be fully known, and that all the Gentiles might hear: and I was delivered out of the mouth of the lion. And the Lord shall deliver me from every evil work, and will preserve me unto his heavenly kingdom: to whom be glory for ever and ever. Amen.*

Paul said, "The Lord stood with me." God is standing with you. Trust Him; believe Him, for He is able. In the school of loneliness we learn that we are never alone or forsaken. Our God is with us.

CHAPTER THIRTEEN

THE PEOPLE NEED A CAPTAIN

avid was destined for the throne of Israel. He was to become the king. In Israel, God worked through David to make Himself known to His people. Also, through Israel, God made Himself known to the rest of the world.

Remember the story given to us about the prophet Samuel going to Bethlehem to the house of David. David lived there with his father, Jesse, and with his brothers and sisters. The prophet Samuel anointed David to be king over Israel. From the time of David's anointing to the time when he actually reigned over Israel as king, many trials came into David's life. God has a definite way of preparing people for what He has prepared for them to do.

Most people think that what they are going through is for the most part without meaning or significance. We will learn someday, as we look back on our lives, that all things work together for our good and God's glory. He allows certain things to touch our lives because His design is to teach us to be a help, an encouragement, and a blessing to others by telling them that our God is able.

In the twenty-second chapter of I Samuel, we find David on the run, going back to the area near where he lived as a boy. The Bible says in I Samuel 22:1-4,

> *David therefore departed thence, and escaped to the cave Adullam: and when his brethren and all his father's house heard it, they went down thither to him. And every one that was in distress, and every one that was in debt, and every one that was discontented, gathered themselves unto him; and he became a captain over them: and there were with him about four hundred men. And David went thence to Mizpeh of Moab: and he said unto the king of Moab, Let my father and my mother, I pray thee, come forth, and be with you, till I know what God will do for me.*

After being introduced to those who were distressed, debtors, and discontented, the Bible declares that David became a captain over them. The people needed a captain.

David became a captain over those who were in distress, over those who were in debt, and over those who were discontented. God did an amazing thing from the four hundred people who gathered themselves around David. All of them were distressed, debtors, and discontented; yet God raised up, from these men, the mightiest army ever known to Israel. The exploits of this particular army under David are talked about to this very day. God did an amazing thing with them when David became their captain. Our God is great!

Did you know that all people have something in common? Everyone needs the Lord. Among all of us who need the Lord, there are two groups: those who know they need Him, and those who do not know they need Him.

The truth is, everyone needs the Lord; some people just do not know it yet. Among those who know they need Him, there are two groups: those who will act upon that need and trust Him for what they need, and those who simply think about how bad off they are and how much they need God, yet never act upon that need.

This crowd came together and rallied around David. He became their captain. In the Bible, we find Old Testament pictures of New Testament truths. David is often a picture, or type, of the Lord Jesus Christ. The Lord Jesus is the captain of our faith. People should rally around Him like these distressed, debtors, and discontented rallied around David. The Lord Jesus Christ is waiting

God has a definite way of preparing people for what He has prepared for them to do.

for us to come unto Him. As a matter of fact, He declared, *"Come unto me, all ye that labour and are heavy laden, and I will give you rest."* Just as David made himself available to those four hundred on that day, the Lord Jesus Christ makes Himself available to all of us.

In the ninth chapter of Matthew, we catch a glimpse into the heart of our Lord. In verses thirty-five through thirty-eight, the Bible says,

> *And Jesus went about all the cities and villages, teaching in their synagogues, and preaching the gospel of the kingdom, and healing every sickness and every disease among the people. But when he saw the multitudes, he was moved with compassion on them, because they fainted, and were scattered abroad, as sheep having no shepherd. Then saith he unto his disciples, The harvest truly is plenteous, but the labourers are few; pray ye therefore the Lord of the harvest, that he will send forth labourers into his harvest.*

The Bible says when the Lord Jesus saw the people, His heart was moved with compassion. He said they were like sheep that had no shepherd, or no captain. Does it occur to you that whatever you are going through, God wants to go through it with you?

David was on the run. He went near Bethlehem and found a hole in the earth, which we call a cave. It was a place of refuge. When these people heard that David was in the land of Judah, they started coming to him. By the time they had finished, four hundred of them had gathered around David, and he became their captain. They desperately needed leadership.

The Lord is the answer. We need to allow Him to be our captain. If you have never trusted Him as your Savior, you need to ask Him to forgive your sin and by faith receive Him as your Savior.

THE CAPTAIN AND HIS FAMILY

In I Samuel 22:1 the Bible says, *"David therefore departed thence, and escaped to the cave Adullam: and when his brethren and all his father's house heard it, they went down thither to him."*

In the story of David and Goliath, remember that David showed up at the camp when Goliath was taunting the army of Israel. For forty days, Goliath went down and mocked God and all of God's people. Do you remember that when David arrived, his brothers became angry with him? They had a family feud over his coming. His oldest brother said, "I know why you are here. You came out here just to see the battle and to show off." Of course, God used David to deliver Israel from that Philistine giant.

After the victory over the giant, David's troubles began. His heart was broken, and King Saul chased him like a wild animal trying to kill him. During David's trouble, his family forgot about all those past problems. They gathered around him. David was glad to see anyone who would be a companion to him. From what I know about life, I am sure that David was especially happy to have his own family by his side.

I have read the life story of D. L. Moody several times. Moody was a famous American evangelist. He had only an elementary education. He yielded his life to God and God used him in a miraculous way. It is said that he took two continents, one in each hand, and shook both continents for the Lord's glory. D. L. Moody had trouble in his home with his son, Will. In a letter Moody wrote to his son, he stated, "My greatest sorrow in life is that you have turned from the God that I love so dearly." There is no hurt quite like hurt in your home.

Alongside Moody's life, in that particular era, was another very famous man by the name of Robert Ingersoll. He was the most well known American atheist of his day. It might interest you to know that Ingersoll grew up in a Presbyterian minister's home. In 1899, Robert Ingersoll and D. L. Moody both died. Ingersoll died in July, and Moody died in December. Of course, the papers in that day picked up on the fact that both of these men died in that year, just before the turn of the

I never cease to be amazed at what God can do with one life.

century. One said that Moody gave all of his life bringing men to light and life. The other man gave all of his life to destroying all the life and light, and bringing in as much darkness as he could.

I will guarantee you that in the Ingersoll family there was a Presbyterian minister whose heart was broken because of what his boy grew up to become. I thank God that there was a day when Moody's boy came back to God and stood by his father's side to serve the Lord. That son left us a wonderful record of his father's life in the biography he authored.

Throughout all of life, it is good to have your family, but it is especially good when things are going rough to have your family by your side. If you have something wrong today in your home, I pray that you will make it right with God and with your family before it takes some great tragedy or heartache to wake you up and bring you to your senses.

THE CAPTAIN AND HIS FOLLOWERS

The Bible says in I Samuel 22:2, *"And every one that was in distress, and every one that was in debt, and every one that was discontented, gathered themselves unto him; and he became a captain over them: and there were with him about four hundred men."*

> *Let me tell you a little secret. I do my best in prayer when I am facing my worst in life.*

These were his followers. I never cease to be amazed at what God can do with one life. Sometimes we get "turned off" by certain people. If we are not careful, we start selecting people and disqualifying others. We say, "Here is someone who can do something, and here is someone who can't do anything with his life. Here is someone who will become something wonderful, and here is someone who will become absolutely nothing." God makes a point of telling us that David's army began with those who were distressed.

Have you ever been distressed? Do you know what distress does? It makes you think. Those people needed a leader. Many people have come to Christ and been saved because of distress. I wonder how many of you who have come to the Lord, asked God to forgive your sin, and trusted Jesus Christ as your Savior, came to God in an hour of great need? Often, when people have problems, they find their way to the Lord Jesus.

God says that these distressed people found their way to David. He became their captain. People who were in debt also found their way to David. People who were discontented found their way to David. If we combine those three words, we cover a world of people: the distressed, the debtors, and the discontented. These words described David and his followers.

Let me tell you a little secret. I do my best in prayer when I am facing my worst in life. When David became king and got in trouble with Bathsheba, he had not been the man of prayer he was in that cave running from Saul. There are things that God allows in life to get our attention.

THE CAPTAIN AND HIS FAITH

David had faith in God. In I Samuel 22:3 the Bible says, *"And David went thence to Mizpeh of Moab: and he said unto the king of Moab, Let my father and my mother, I pray thee, come forth, and be with you, till I know what God will do for me."*

David did a very tender thing when he took his parents to the king of Moab. He told the king, "I want you to know that Saul is trying to kill me. I fear for my mother and father, and for my family. I want you to take care of them."

If you remember the book of Ruth in the Old Testament, you recall that Ruth was a Moabitess. She married a man by the name of Boaz. They had a son named Obed. Obed had a son named Jesse. Jesse had a family, and one of his sons was named David. David's great-grandfather was married to someone from Moab. When Naomi and Ruth came back from Moab, there was another girl by the name of Orpah who stayed behind. She had been married to Naomi's son,

151

Mahlon. She stayed in Moab. In all probability she still had relatives around that area. David sought relatives in Moab to care for his mother and father.

He traveled to Moab and desired the king to care for his family. For how long? Here is what I want you to see. David said, *"Till I know what God will do for me."* He said, "I don't know how long it will last, but my faith is in God, and I know that God will see me through this." We all need that kind of faith in God.

The person with faith in God does not know all the answers, but he knows God. Faith in God cannot see the beginning from the end.

> *The person with faith in God does not know all the answers, but he knows God.*

You do not know how it is going to work out, but you know that God is going to work it out. We need faith in God.

In I Peter 5:8, the Bible speaks of the Devil desiring to devour people. Satan walks about as a roaring lion, seeking whom he may devour. In the same context, the Bible says in I Peter 5:7, *"Casting all your care upon him; for he careth for you."* In other words, give it all to the Lord because He cares for you. Dear friend, cast your cares on the Lord!

David had been told he would be the king of Israel. He was forced to flee like an animal from Saul. He was hiding in a cave, and when the people heard he was there, four hundred who were distressed, and debtors, and discontented gathered around him. He had his own family to care for, and gladly he cared for them. What was he going to do in the midst of all that difficulty? He decided, "I will wait *'till I know what God will do for me.'"*

I would to God that every one of us had that kind of faith in the Lord. When I think about the things I am responsible for and all the needs I have, I think, "Lord, I am not able." But God is able. We must give it all to Him.

We all need a captain, and we know it. Our captain is Christ! Bring your needs to Him and say, "Lord, help me." He will. Cast your cares on Him.

When I was fourteen years old, a man asked me, "Are you a Christian?" I said, "I think so," and I told him why I thought I was. I believed in God. I was trying to do as good as I could. If I got behind, I planned to catch up before death. I thought that one day God would put all the good things I did on one side and all the bad things I did on the other side. I thought that if I did more good than I did bad, God would let me into heaven. It just does not work that way. I was a sinner, just like you are a sinner. We are all sinners. Christ died for our sins. He rose from the dead.

That man explained to me that I had to ask God to forgive my sin. He told me that I must trust Jesus Christ as my personal Savior. I prayed and asked God to forgive my sin, and I invited the Lord into my life. From that day to this, I have had a Captain. I have not always followed Him as I should, but I have a Captain to lead me. I need my Captain every day. He is available to all who know Him as their Savior. Trust Him now.